A COLLINGRIDGE
START-RIGHT BOOK

Starting with Roses

Nothing could illustrate better the true value of roses as garden flowers than the author's comment that some eight million British gardeners grow them and that something like four million rose bushes are bought in this country every year. Mr A. G. L. Hellyer also puts his finger on the reason for this incredible popularity when he says that 'the best roses today will keep a garden beautiful for a longer period and for less outlay in time and money than any other plant'. In fact, one can say without fear of contradiction that the rose is the ideal beginner's flower. So great, too, is the fascination of roses that many newcomers to rose growing find that their interest in these plants stays with them for a lifetime.

As Editor of *Amateur Gardening* Mr Hellyer is more conversant than most gardening authorities with the problems and aspirations of the keen amateur gardener. His practical experience of rose growing extends over more than 40 years, and his professional duties have given him unrivalled opportunities to observe and assess the activities of those rose breeders and nurserymen who have brought the modern garden rose to the pitch of perfection it has undoubtedly reached today.

In logical progression, Mr Hellyer takes the reader through every phase of rose cultivation. His information is clear and to the point, completely up to date and totally devoid of verbiage. The soil and its improvement; siting a rose garden; the classification of roses and choosing varieties; the use of roses; planting, pruning, exhibiting, propagation and controlling pests and diseases—these are the subjects discussed by Mr Hellyer. His text, together with many colour and black and white illustrations, make *Starting With Roses* the perfect introduction to these most beautiful and adaptable garden flowers.

A COLLINGRIDGE
START-RIGHT BOOK

Starting with Roses

A. G. L. HELLYER, F.L.S.

W. H. & L. COLLINGRIDGE LTD
LONDON

First published in 1966
by W. H. & L. Collingridge Limited
Tower House Southampton Street London WC2
Printed in Great Britain by
Hazell Watson & Viney Limited
Aylesbury Bucks

Contents

Illustrations

Colour Plates

(All colour plates reproduced by kind permission of R. and G. Cuthbert Ltd.)

Monochrome Plates

Line-drawings

CHAPTER ONE

Making the Most of One's Opportunities

The rose has fascinated gardeners with its fragrance and beauty for thousands of years, but it is only in the twentieth century that it has become the most popular of garden plants. It owes this advancement to improvements built into it by breeders who have sought to widen its colour range, strengthen its constitution and extend its flowering season. In all these matters they have been so successful that the best roses today will keep a garden beautiful for a longer period and for less outlay in time and money than any other plant. No wonder that eight million gardeners in Britain grow roses and that something like four million buy rose bushes every year. How many are doing so for the first time the figures do not disclose, but the number must be considerable and it is for such gardeners that this book is primarily designed.

SOIL REQUIREMENTS

For the majority of would-be rosarians the selection of the plot of land upon which to commence operations is strictly limited. In most cases they are already provided with a garden. Even when this is not the case, few are in a position to select their dwelling-place mainly with a view to the welfare of their roses. So I will not waste time by discussing the ideal rose garden, which scarcely exists outside the dreams of authors, but will rather seek to show how the most unpromising sites can be turned to good account and made to produce surprisingly fine roses.

It is generally understood that roses appreciate a deep, rather heavy loam, not waterlogged or sour, but well supplied with plant foods, and stiff enough to allow the long, thongy roots, typical of wild English brier stock upon which most roses are grown, to get a satisfactory hold and congenial cool run. It is not so widely known that many of our leading and most successful growers have to produce their plants and blooms under conditions quite contrary to these. They, too, have been faced with the necessity of making the most of what they possessed, and their success should be an encouragement to any beginner who feels that he has little chance of excelling because his garden is not composed of just the sort of soil which he has been given to understand is essential.

The truth is that by the aid of proper cultivation and the judicious application of manures and other substances almost any garden in the British Isles can be made to produce quite satisfactory roses. If, in addition, a little attention is given to the selection of suitable varieties worked upon stocks adapted to the nature of the soil, one may even expect to see gardeners in most unlikely districts blossoming forth as prize-winners.

The Importance of Humus

It is a good plan, before commencing to cultivate any plant, to get an idea of its basic likes and dislikes. For example, one may lay it down at the start that roses do not like being dried out, yet appreciate a sufficiency of sun to ensure thorough ripening of the wood. The more open the beds are to light and air, the easier will be the gardener's task, but if the soil is of a dry nature, it must have sufficient organic matter, or 'humus', added to it to ensure that, even after a long hot spell, it will not become parched and cracked.

Thus humus may be provided in a variety of ways. The commonest and best is well-rotted farmyard manure that has a liberal amount of straw in its composition. Unfortunately, this is not readily obtained near a town, and haulage over long distances may make the price prohibitive. Stable manure is the next best thing. Samples containing wood shavings in considerable quantity should be avoided, as they nearly always give rise to fungus growths, while their mechanical effect in rendering the soil more retentive of moisture is not to be compared with samples containing a straw foundation. Sawdust, however, is not unsatisfactory as a bedding material mixed with manure, for it decays fairly rapidly and then makes good humus. Any decayed vegetable matter may be used with advantage if well worked in. Lawn mowings and other garden refuse stacked in an out-of-the-way place will rot down into quite a good organic manure, or by the use of one of the advertised rotting compounds can be converted into an even better substitute for farmyard manure. Another simple scheme is to build the refuse into a heap about 3 feet high, as much through and of any convenient length. As each 6-inch layer is piled on to this heap it is dusted lightly with Nitro-chalk. Any dry portions of refuse are wetted thoroughly. After a month the heap is turned and wetted again, if dry. In three months it should be well rotted and ready for use, and will prove almost as good as animal manure.

Spent hops offer another excellent means of supplying light soils with this much-needed humus, while the refuse from tanyards, consisting largely of hair scraped from the skins, is very beneficial. Shoddy, which is the refuse from wool factories, has a similar value in opening and improving the soil.

Old rotted turves are also of great value to the rose grower. Turf can frequently be obtained quite cheaply from building sites and should be secured whenever possible. Indeed, there is really no better staple for the rose-beds than good, fibrous, top-spit soil.

Peat is a most valuable source of humus and has the added recommendation that it is easily available. Either sphagnum peat or sedge peat may be used and, if several grades are available, a fairly coarse one should be chosen as this will open the soil more effectively than a fine, dusty peat. Usually peat is purchased dry and it must then be well wetted before it is mixed with the soil, as dry peat tends to reject moisture whereas damp peat accepts it readily and acts like a sponge. So if the peat arrives in a polythene bag, simply open this and pour in as much water as it will conveniently take. Then leave it for 24 hours for the water to soak in. If the peat comes in compressed bales, break these open, spread out the peat in some convenient place, water it generously, and then throw it into a heap and leave for 24 hours.

The mechanical action of all the foregoing substances can best be likened to a sponge. During extremely wet weather they tend to keep the soil open and prevent waterlogging, while in a dry spell they slowly give off the moisture they have absorbed, at the same time preventing the rapid evaporation of water from lower levels. In this way they act as moisture regulators, and the gardener who has made sure that his soil is liberally supplied with humus has overcome half his drainage problems.

The Treatment of Heavy Soils

Humus is as valuable on heavy soils as it is upon that which is too light and quickly drained. But in such cases preference should be given to the lighter organic manures, such as peat, the refuse from tanyards, shoddy, spent hops and stable manure. Pig and cow manure, unless they are very well decomposed or contain an abundance of straw, are liable to make a stiff clay soil even colder and more retentive of moisture.

Nearly all clay soil becomes even heavier a foot or so below the surface. Though it is wise to break this stodgy sub-stratum up as much as possible, it is not a good plan to bring it to the surface where it would merely become baked by the sun into brick-like lumps.

Drainage may be effected by cutting trenches 18 to 24 inches deep and 12 inches wide with a slight fall to a large soak-away. This is constructed by excavating a hole of suitable size—say about 5 feet square by 4 feet deep to drain an area of 4 or 5 rods of ground—and filling it with clinkers and large stones, finishing off with layers of smaller stones, ashes and inverted turves. The trenches should have a layer of large clinkers 9 inches deep or a row of earthenware land-drain pipes at the bottom, and should then be filled with smaller clinkers or stones, and eventually soil. Surplus water will thus be collected and carried to the soak-away, from which it will gradually percolate into the subsoil.

The Improvement of Chalky Land

Perhaps the greatest problem of all is presented on poor, chalky land. Even this, by good cultivation and suitable planting can be made into a satisfactory rose garden. Decomposed organic matter will be invaluable, while meadow loam, old turves, or other similar material that will give body to the soil should be used if available. Peat is a particularly good dressing for chalk land, for it is usually acid in reaction and so tends to counteract the excessive alkalinity produced by the chalk. Roses appear to thrive best on a soil that is either neutral or a little on the acid side. When land is markedly alkaline in reaction the leaves of roses often become yellow in patches, a condition known as chlorosis.

Stones are not Detrimental

Those who are faced with very rubbly soils frequently fall into the error of going to a tremendous amount of trouble to remove all possible stones. This is unnecessary. Very large stones must be taken out as they make it difficult to work soil and are likely to cause broken tools, but smaller stones do more good than harm. During hot weather they condense quite a lot of water on their lower surfaces, a fact which may readily be proved if a fair-sized stone be turned over at the end of a warm summer's day. In wet weather stones help to hold soil open and allow surplus water to escape, so they perform a double function.

Siting a Rose Garden

The ideal situation for a rose garden is one that is open and sunny. A few roses grow well in shade but most tend to be weakened to some extent by it. Overhanging branches of trees are bad because they not only cut off the light but they tend to keep the roses too dry. Some shelter, especially on the north and east, may be beneficial, though most modern roses are very tough and hardy, but too much enclosure is bad as it prevents free movement of air and encourages such diseases as mildew.

One rather odd thing is that roses grown in and near towns, particularly towns where there are many factories, often suffer far less from disease, and, in particular, from one very troublesome disease known as black spot, than roses grown in the country. This appears to be because the smoke-polluted air contains chemicals, probably sulphur compounds, which kill the fungi which cause black spot and some other diseases.

This is a pleasant bonus for the town gardener, who often feels at a disadvantage. In fact, with roses, he appears to be better placed than a great many country gardeners and some of the finest rose gardens are in or near large towns.

CHAPTER TWO

The Different Kinds of Roses

Most of the roses grown in gardens today are highly complex man-made hybrids but all have been evolved from wild roses, or species. However, roses have been grown by gardeners for so many centuries that the beginning of it all is lost in antiquity and the experts can only guess which wild roses were first used.

Today we know about 200 species of roses but only a very few of these have been used in producing the garden hybrids. Some of these wild roses are beautiful plants, well worth growing in gardens, but most of them have a comparatively short flowering season and many make big bushes, two characteristics which render them unsuitable for mass planting in beds. Their proper place is in the shrub border or planted in isolation as specimen bushes.

The same short flowering season is characteristic of all the garden hybrid roses up to the early part of the nineteenth century. Some entirely new roses were then introduced from the Far East. The first to arrive were known as China roses and their origin is a little obscure, but they were probably ancient hybrids between *Rosa chinensis* and *R. odorata*, two wild Chinese roses. A few years later *R. odorata* itself followed. What all these roses had in common was the habit of flowering continuously more or less all the summer. This was an entirely new, and very welcome, quality which gardeners quickly appreciated and sought to breed into the roses they already had. Soon there were two distinct races of roses with an extended flowering season. The Tea roses, so called because they had a curious tea-like perfume, were the most persistent in flowering but they were not very hardy and they lacked the more intense rose colours. The Hybrid Perpetuals, by contrast, did not flower so continuously, despite their name, but they had bigger, fuller flowers in a greater range of colours.

The obvious thing was to cross these two races together and so

Rose Gaujard (HT)

Sutter's Gold (HT)

Anne Letts (HT)

Cleopatra (HT)

Grandpa Dickson (HT)

Sterling Silver (HT)

Ena Harkness
(HT)

attempt to combine the best features of each in a new race. This was done and the Hybrid Tea rose was produced. It remains to this day the standard of perfection so far as flower quality is concerned, but for freedom and continuity of flower it has been surpassed by another even more modern race, the Floribunda. Varieties of this type usually produce their flowers in larger clusters than those of the Hybrid Tea roses, though individually the flowers are smaller, and the best Floribunda roses really do bloom almost without break from June to October.

The dividing line between Hybrid Tea and Floribunda becomes more blurred each year because of persistent interbreeding between the two races, and it would not be surprising if in a few years time a new grouping has to be sought. Already for many purposes it is more convenient to think of bedding roses and cutting (or exhibition) roses than it is of Floribundas and Hybrid Teas.

Rose catalogues, besides listing many varieties in each of these two great groups, also have other important classes of roses. There will be Climbing Roses, which will include a variety of roses, some raised specifically as climbers, and some derived from ordinary bush varieties which have produced extra vigorous forms, or 'sports'. These latter, by the rules of nomenclature, always bear the name of the variety from which they have been derived, prefixed by the word 'climbing'. Thus Climbing Ena Harkness is a very vigorous sport of the crimson Hybrid Tea rose Ena Harkness, and resembles it exactly in flower. By contrast Danse de Feu is a bright red rose which, though of Hybrid Tea origin, had sufficient vigour to be regarded as a climber from the moment it appeared as a new seedling. The distinction is of more than academic interest since the pruning of climbing sports follows slightly different lines from that of climbers, a matter discussed in the chapter on pruning (p. 52).

Then there are Rambler roses which make long, rather thin stems, the natural tendency of which is to trail or ramble. They can be allowed to do just that, and are excellent for covering banks, but more usually they are trained upwards on trellis work or walls or over pergolas and arches.

There are Dwarf Polyantha roses which have something in common with ramblers for, like them, their flowers, usually quite small individually, are produced in large clusters. They were the

1. A Climbing rose.   *2. A Rambler rose*

forerunners of the Floribunda roses which were produced by crossing Dwarf Polyantha roses with Hybrid Tea roses and they have, to a very considerable extent, been superseded by Floribunda varieties. Nevertheless, they are still good roses in their own right and a few varieties are still listed by most nurserymen.

Miniature roses might be described as super-dwarf Polyanthas. They only grow 9 to 12 inches high and have little pompon flowers to match. Mostly they are grown as small pot plants or in the rock garden but some varieties can be used as edgings to beds.

Shrub rose is a term applied to almost any bush rose that is too big to grow comfortably in a bed along with a lot of other similar roses. Some catalogues make a separate classification for Hybrid

3. *A Floribunda rose.* 4. *Hybrid Tea rose.*
5 *An Old-fashioned rose*

Musk roses, which are supposed to be derived from a species named *Rosa moschata*, but the present tendency is to lump the Hybrid Musk roses along with the Shrub roses and this seems entirely sensible as most of them make big bushes which fit well into the shrub garden.

Some catalogues also make a separate class for Old-fashioned roses, a rather vague term which may include not only the genuinely old roses but even some twentieth-century varieties that look like old roses. Since a great many of these are vigorous bush roses which flower only once each year, in June or July, it is convenient to consider them as Shrub roses. Alternatively, an opposite course may be taken and the Old-fashioned roses may be listed under the various class names they originally bore; e.g. as Moss roses, Cabbage roses, Damask roses, Noisette roses, Bourbon roses, Gallica roses, etc., but nowadays this is only likely to be done by nurserymen who specialise in these antique varieties.

One other distinction needs to be made plain which has nothing to do with the parentage or origin of the roses. Catalogues offer 'bush' roses, 'standard' roses, 'weeping standard' roses and, occasionally, 'half-standard' roses. These terms apply to the form in which the rose is grown. 'Bush' speaks for itself. It is a form which starts to branch more or less from ground level. A 'standard', by contrast, has a bare stem at least 3½ feet long on top of which is a head of branches. The 'half-standard' is similar but the bare stem is 3 feet or less in height. The 'weeping standard' has a much longer stem, usually 5 to 5½ feet, on which is grown, not a bushy type of rose, but one of the Rambler roses, the thin stems of which hang down almost to ground level.

Because all this may seem a little confusing to anyone new to rose growing, I have attempted to sum it all up in a simple table:

HYBRID TEA	Roses with large, shapely flowers produced singly or in small clusters. In flower intermittently from June to October.
FLORIBUNDA	Roses with small- to medium-size flowers produced in medium to large clusters. In flower almost continually from June to October.
CLIMBERS	Roses with long, fairly stiff stems and medium to large flowers. Some flower once only, some intermittently most of the summer.
RAMBLER	Roses with very long flexible stems and small flowers in large clusters. Bloom once only each year, usually in July.
SHRUB	Roses with small- to medium-size flowers, produced singly or in clusters. A good branching habit and sturdy stems 5 feet or more in height.
OLD-FASHIONED	Any rose raised before the twentieth century or with the appearance characteristic of these old roses.

DWARF
   POLYANTHA

MIINIATURE

Bushy roses 1 to 3 feet high with small flowers in clusters. Flowering from June to October.

Roses 1 foot or less in height with very small flowers in clusters. Flowering from June to October.

CHAPTER THREE

Choosing Varieties

It is no easy matter for one rose grower to make a selection for another, still less for the writer of a book, which may be on sale for some years, to give advice on this matter. Even if he succeeds in catering for the varied requirements of all his readers he can still do nothing to keep abreast of the flood of new varieties that appear every year. It often takes several years for a new rose to settle down and show its worth and there is also the possibility that excellent varieties will develop faults as they age.

Keep Up To Date

Therefore, before proceeding further to give lists of roses for various purposes I must impress upon my readers the advisability of checking these against the latest lists. The catalogues issued by trade specialists are as a rule excellent except for a tendency to run wild in colour descriptions. When you read that a rose combines shades of vermilion, copper, salmon and yellow, learn to make due allowances and to realise that though each of these colours may be present at certain stages in development and in certain parts of the bloom, the general effect to the casual eye will probably be just a bright red.

The Royal National Rose Society issues an admirable *Annual*, which, among other excellent features, includes a yearly analysis of the best roses for various purposes. In addition, it publishes from time to time a *Select List of Roses*. These are sent free of charge to members, and are themselves well worth the annual subscription of half a guinea. Needless to say, there are many other benefits of membership, including free admission to all the society's shows in London and the provinces. I strongly advise all keen rose growers to join.

See Roses in Growth and Bloom

Even after gathering information from all these sources, and possibly visiting one or two rose shows, it is desirable to see the fancied varieties in growth and bloom before making a final decision. This should not be difficult. Most cities and large towns have excellent public parks where good collections of modern roses are grown. Londoners can visit the Queen Mary Rose Garden in Regent's Park, which is a model of what such a garden should be. In addition, there are good rose nurseries in all parts of the country. Nursery collections are naturally more complete and up to date than those in most gardens or parks, but they do suffer from one rather serious drawback. They are composed entirely of maiden roses—i.e. roses in their first season of growth. Cases are not unknown of varieties which grow well and flower freely as maidens, but do little good in subsequent years. Fortunately this does not apply to the majority of roses; in fact, only to a quite small minority.

Some rose nurserymen have made excellent display gardens in which plants are allowed to grow on from year to year and develop exactly as they would in a park or private garden. These display gardens have the added merit that they are usually kept right up to date with varieties, many of which it might be difficult to see elsewhere.

SELECT LISTS OF VARIETIES

Without making any claim that the following lists of varieties are in any way exhaustive or that they are the best in each class, I do think that they may be helpful to those who have nothing but the printed word to guide them. They are all roses which I know from personal observation to be good of their kind and capable of giving satisfaction under ordinary garden conditions.

HYBRID TEAS

Anne Letts.   Large, well-shaped, soft pink flowers, very fragrant. Medium height, branching habit.

Anne Watkins.   Well-shaped apricot flowers paling to cream. Moderately fragrant. Medium height.

Ballet. A very full flower, clear pink in colour with moderate fragrance. Medium height and good, branching habit. Very prolific, making a good show in the garden.

Beauté. Yellow flushed with apricot, flowers full and well shaped with some fragrance. Medium height, bushy habit.

Blue Moon. Shapely lavender-blue flowers, nicely fragrant. Medium height and branching habit.

Buccaneer. Medium-sized deep yellow flowers. Moderate fragrance. Rather tall habit.

Christian Dior. A shapely, bright scarlet rose with little fragrance. The young leaves are coppery coloured and attractive. Medium height, branching habit.

Cleopatra. Large, full flowers, currant red with gold reverse. Slight fragrance. Medium height.

Dorothy Peach. Large, full, yellow flowers with moderate fragrance. Medium height and branching habit.

Eden Rose. A very glowing pink with even brighter reverse. A big, full, shapely rose with a good fragrance. Medium height, branching habit.

Ena Harkness. A shapely, full-petalled, bright crimson rose with moderate fragrance. Medium height and bushy habit.

Fragrant Cloud. Large, very full, geranium-lake flowers, powerfully scented and freely produced. Medium height and bushy habit.

Fritz Thiedemann. Deep salmon to vermilion flowers, shapely, but only moderately fragrant. Medium height and bushy habit.

Gail Borden. Very large, full, bright pink and gold flowers, moderately scented. Medium height and bushy habit.

Gavotte. Light rose-pink flowers, paler outside, full and shapely. Fragrant. Medium height and bushy habit.

Gertrude Gregory. Shapely, full petalled, rich yellow, fragrant flowers of medium size. Rather tall, bushy habit.

Gold Crown. Large, full-petalled, deep yellow flowers. Rather tall, bushy habit.

Grand'mère Jenny. Very large, full, soft yellow flowers flushed with pink. Some fragrance. Tall, bushy habit.

Grandpa Dickson. Large, well-formed, light yellow flowers. Moderate fragrance. Rather vigorous habit.

Josephine Bruce. Shapely, full-petalled, rich crimson flowers with plenty of fragrance. Medium height, bushy habit.

Karl Herbst. Very large, full, light red flowers. Slight fragrance. Medium height.

King's Ransom. Shapely, yellow flowers of medium size, freely produced and with moderate fragrance. Medium to tall, bushy habit.

Lady Belper. Large, full-petalled, shapely, apricot flowers, moderately fragrant. Medium height, bushy habit.

Madame Louis Laperrière. Deepest velvety crimson flowers, richly scented. Rather short, well branched habit.

Margaret. Clear pink with lighter reverse, full, shapely moderately fragrant flowers. Medium height, bushy habit.

McGredy's Yellow. Large, full, light yellow flowers with moderate fragrance. Tall, well branched habit.

Mischief. Medium size, shapely orange and vermilion flowers freely produced and fully fragrant. Medium height, bushy habit.

Mojave. Coppery-orange flowers rather lacking in substance, very sweetly scented. Medium height, bushy habit.

Monique. Deep shell-pink flowers of exquisite shape and with good fragrance. Medium height, bushy habit.

Montezuma. Shapely dusky reddish-salmon blooms. Slightly fragrant. Medium height, bushy habit.

Mrs Sam McGredy. Coppery-orange and rose flowers. Good fragrance. Medium height, bushy habit.

My Choice. Shapely soft carmine and gold flowers, fully fragrant. Medium height, bushy habit.

Opera. Big, full, shapely bright carmine flowers, nicely fragrant. Medium height, bushy habit.

Papa Meilland. Well-shaped deep crimson flowers. Medium height. Very fragrant.

Peace. Very large, full lemon-yellow flowers edged with red. Not much fragrance. Very vigorous, tall and well branched.

Perfecta. Shapely, full-petalled flowers, ivory edged with rose. Not much fragrance. Rather tall, erect habit not much branched.

Piccadilly. Large, shapely orange-scarlet and yellow flowers moderately scented. Medium height, bushy habit.

Picture. Shapely warm pink flowers, only slightly scented. Medium height, bushy habit.

Pink Favourite. Large, full, shapely rose-pink flowers, not much scent. Medium height, bushy habit.

Prima Ballerina. Large, full, shapely pink flowers. Very fragrant. Medium height, branching habit.

Rose Gaujard. Large, full flowers white or cream heavily flushed with carmine. Moderate fragrance. Rather tall, branching habit.

Silver Lining. Large, shapely and full, soft rose flowers paling to white at the base and delightfully fragrant. Medium height, branching habit.

Stella. Large, very shapely carmine flowers shading to near white at the base. A very beautiful rose which has little fragrance. Rather tall, branching habit.

Sterling Silver. Shapely, lavender-lilac flowers, fully fragrant. Medium height, branching habit.

Super Star. Very shapely, full bright vermilion flowers, moderately fragrant. Medium height, branching habit.

Sutter's Gold. Medium size, rich yellow flowers shaded with red, fully fragrant. Rather tall, upright habit.

Tzigane. Orange-red flowers with gold reverse. Moderate fragrance. Medium height.

Virgo. Pure white flowers with large petals. Moderately fragrant. Medium height, bushy habit.

Wendy Cussons. Large, full, shapely deep cerise flowers, richly fragrant. Medium height, branching habit.

Westminster. Deep cherry-red with gold reverse, large, full flowers, fully fragrant. Medium height, branching habit.

FLORIBUNDAS

Allgold. Deep yellow, semi-double, fragrant flowers in good clusters. Medium height.

Anna Wheatcroft. Soft vermilion flowers that are nearly single. Slightly fragrant. Medium height.

Ascot. Rather large, shapely salmon-pink flowers. Dwarf habit.

Chanelle. Shell-pink paling to light peach. Fragrant. Rather tall.

Circus. Flowers yellow at first deepening to orange, flushed with carmine, borne in large clusters. Fragrant. Medium height.

Dearest. Large, sweetly scented salmon-pink flowers. Medium height.

Elizabeth of Glamis. Large, shapely, orange-salmon sweetly scented flowers. Medium height.

Europeana. Blood-red flowers of fair size produced in large clusters. Slightly fragrant. Medium height.

Evelyn Fison. Brilliant scarlet flowers in large clusters. Medium height.

Fashion. Shapely, clear salmon, fragrant flowers. A little below medium height.

Faust. Large, well-formed yellow flowers. Rather tall habit.

Firecracker. Vivid cherry-red and yellow, semi-double flowers in large clusters. Some fragrance. Medium height.

Frensham. Light crimson flowers of good size, very freely produced. Slightly fragrant. Tall and very vigorous.

Highlight. Orange-scarlet, slightly fragrant flowers in large clusters. Medium height.

Honeymoon. Fragrant, canary-yellow roses of good size and substance. Light green foliage. Rather tall habit.

Iceberg. Shapely, pure white flowers very freely produced. Moderately fragrant. Rather thin growth but tall habit.

Korona.   Large, semi-double flame-scarlet flowers, very freely produced. Slightly fragrant. Rather tall habit.

Lilli Marlene.   Rich crimson, slightly scented flowers very freely produced in large clusters. Medium height.

Marlena.   Blood-red flowers very freely produced on a low, well-branched bush.

Masquerade.   Flowers at first yellow, gradually changing through pink to carmine. Slightly fragrant. Freely produced in large clusters. Rather tall and very vigorous.

Orangeade.   Tangerine, semi-double, slightly scented flowers. Rather under medium height.

Orange Sensation.   Fairly large, bright orange-red, fragrant flowers very freely produced. Medium height.

Paddy McGredy.   Large, full, fragrant, shapely deep rose flowers in good clusters. Rather below medium height.

Paprika.   Bright turkey-red flowers in large clusters. Medium height.

Queen Elizabeth.   Large, shapely, slightly fragrant salmon-pink flowers. Very tall, vigorous habit.

Red Favourite.   Large, well formed blood-red flowers in big clusters. Slightly fragrant. Medium height.

Rosemary Rose.   Large, double, flat-topped flowers of currant red with purple foliage. Medium height.

Sarabande.   Intense orange-scarlet single flowers. Medium height.

Shepherd's Delight.   Vermilion flowers shading to yellow in large clusters. Fragrant. Tall habit.

Vera Dalton.   Large, well formed, slightly fragrant, rose-pink flowers. Medium height.

Violet Carson.   Small but shapely pale shrimp-pink flowers. Slight fragrance. Medium height.

Woburn Abbey.   Large, well formed, fragrant, deep orange flowers. Medium height.

CLIMBING ROSES

Allen Chandler. Large, semi-double, scarlet, fragrant flowers freely produced in early summer, with some more in early autumn.

Chaplin's Pink Climber. Fairly large, semi-double, bright pink flowers in large clusters in July.

Climbing Crimson Glory. Large, fully double, fragrant, deep crimson flowers freely produced in early summer, with some more in early autumn.

Climbing Ena Harkness. Large, fully double, fragrant, bright crimson flowers, freely produced in early summer, with some more in early autumn.

Climbing Etoile de Hollande. Large, fully double, very fragrant crimson flowers, freely produced in early summer, with some more in early autumn.

Climbing Golden Dawn. Large, fully double, very fragrant, light yellow flowers, freely produced in early summer, with some more in early autumn.

Climbing Goldilocks. Medium size, fragrant, yellow flowers in clusters all summer.

Climbing Lady Sylvia. Large, fully double, very fragrant pink flowers, freely produced in early summer, with some more in early autumn.

Climbing Madame Butterfly. Large, fully double, very fragrant flowers, freely produced in early summer, with some more in early autumn.

Climbing Madame Caroline Testout. Very large fully double, slightly fragrant pink flowers, freely produced in early summer, with some more in early autumn.

Climbing Madame Edouard Herriot. Large, fully double terra-cotta flowers, freely produced in early summer, with some more in early autumn.

Climbing Mrs Sam McGredy. Large, double, fragrant, coppery-orange and rose flowers, freely produced in early summer, with some more in early autumn.

Climbing Shot Silk. Large, fully double, very fragrant, bright pink and gold flowers, freely produced in early summer, with some more in early autumn.

Danse de Feu. Medium size, double, orange-scarlet flowers all summer.

Elegance. Large, shapely, double yellow flowers, mainly in June and July. Slight fragrance.

Golden Showers. Large, fully double, fragrant yellow flowers all summer.

Madame Gregoire Staechelin. Large, double, very fragrant carmine and pink flowers in June and July.

Meg. Single or semi-double, apricot and pink flowers in large clusters intermittently in summer.

Mermaid. Large, single, soft yellow, fragrant flowers all summer.

Parkdirektor Riggers. Large, semi-double, blood-red flowers all summer.

Paul's Lemon Pillar. Very large, double, ivory, fragrant flowers in June and July.

Paul's Scarlet Climber. Fairly large, double, scarlet flowers in large clusters in July.

Royal Gold. Large, double, deep yellow, fragrant flowers all summer.

Zéphirine Drouhin. Large, double, fragrant, clear pink flowers all summer. Thornless.

RAMBLER ROSES

Alberic Barbier. Double, creamy-white, fragrant flowers in June. Nearly evergreen leaves.

Albertine. Fairly large, coppery-pink, very fragrant flowers in June.

American Pillar. Single, rose and white flowers in large clusters in July.

Crimson Shower. Semi-double crimson flowers in large clusters throughout late summer.

Dorothy Perkins. Small, shell-pink flowers in large clusters in July.

Dr W. van Fleet. Fairly large, pale pink, fragrant flowers in July.

Emily Gray. Fairly large, double, apricot flowers in June. Beautiful glossy foliage.

Excelsa. Small, double, crimson flowers in large clusters in July and August.

New Dawn. Very like Dr W. van Fleet, but flowers all summer.

Sanders' White. Small, double, fragrant, white flowers in large clusters in July and August.

Violette. Small, double, lavender-purple flowers in large clusters in July.

SHRUB ROSES

Blanc Double de Coubert. Semi-double, very fragrant, white flowers all summer, 6 feet.

Bonn. Large, double, light scarlet flowers with musk fragrance, all summer, 5 feet.

Celestial. Double, shell-pink, fragrant flowers in June and July, grey-green leaves, 7 feet.

Chinatown. Large, double, light yellow slightly fragrant flowers all summer, 6 feet.

Cornelia. Double, rose-pink and salmon, very fragrant flowers in clusters all summer, 5 feet.

Elmshorn. Double, rose-pink and salmon, fragrant flowers in clusters all summer, 5 feet.

Felicia. Double, shell-pink, very fragrant flowers in large clusters all summer, 5 feet.

Frühlingsgold. Large, semi-double, fragrant, creamy-yellow flowers in June, 8 feet.

Frühlingsmorgen. Large, single, cream and pink flowers in June, 6 feet.

Kassel. Semi-double, cherry-red flowers in large clusters all summer, 5 feet.

Madame Hardy.   Large, double, very fragrant, white flowers in June and July, 6 feet.

Magenta.   Large, double, very fragrant, lilac-purple flowers all summer, 4 feet.

Maiden's Blush.   Double, fragrant, flesh-pink flowers in June and July, 5 feet.

Maigold.   Large, semi-double, fragrant, deep yellow flowers all summer, 7 feet.

Nevada.   Large, semi-double, creamy-white flowers produced in June, with some more in August or September, 7 feet.

Penelope.   Semi-double, pale apricot-pink, fragrant flowers all summer, 6 feet.

Prosperity.   Pink buds opening to double, white, fragrant flowers all summer, 6 feet.

Rosa cantabrigiensis.   Single, soft yellow flowers in May and June, 8 feet.

Rosa gallica versicolor.   Semi-double, red flowers freely striped with white, June flowering, 3 feet.

Rosa moyesii Geranium.   Single, crimson flowers in June, followed by large, bottle-shaped, scarlet hips, 8 feet.

Rosa rubrifolia.   Small, single, rose-pink flowers in June. Blue-grey leaves tinged with pink and purple, 7 feet.

Rosa xanthina spontanea. (Canary Bird).   Small, single, bright yellow flowers in May, 6 feet.

Scarlet Fire.   Large, single, bright scarlet flowers in June or July, 7 feet.

Wilhelm.   Double, light crimson, slightly fragrant flowers in large clusters all the summer, 6 feet.

Piccadilly (HT)

Peace (HT)

Papa Meilland (HT)

Margaret (HT)

Dorothy Peach (HT)

Anne Watkins (HT)

Super Star (HT)

CHAPTER FOUR

Planning the Rose Beds

Though roses can be used to beautify the smallest of areas and may be associated quite successfully with other plants, it is in a separate bed—or, better still, series of beds—that they are seen to the best advantage. If the gardener can possibly set aside a plot, even though quite small, entirely for his roses, he will certainly be rewarded, not only by better individual blooms, but also by a much more effective general display.

Aspects of Design

The design of the rose garden will be determined by personal taste. No general rules can be laid down except, perhaps, the purely practical one that very small or narrow beds are difficult to plant effectively and very large or wide ones are difficult to work. A bed 5 feet wide will accommodate three rows of roses and, if there is access from both sides, it will be possible to keep it free of weeds and to tend the roses with a minimum of walking on the soil. Two rows can just be accommodated in a 3-feet wide bed and 18 inches is the absolute minimum for one row.

Some people like beds arranged in formal patterns, as in the accompanying plan, others will prefer a much simpler arrangement. In a long garden, a section for roses may be used to break it up into more pleasing proportions and rose hedges or screens may be used to emphasise the division. The rose-covered arch is a useful device to give height to an otherwise flat design and, where space permits, the rose-covered pergola provides similar relief on a larger scale.

A sunken rose garden, enclosed by low retaining walls, can look charming but before constructing one it is wise to make sure that it will not become a water trap in winter. There are few things roses dislike more than having their roots in waterlogged soil for long periods. Sometimes the effect of a sunken garden can be obtained

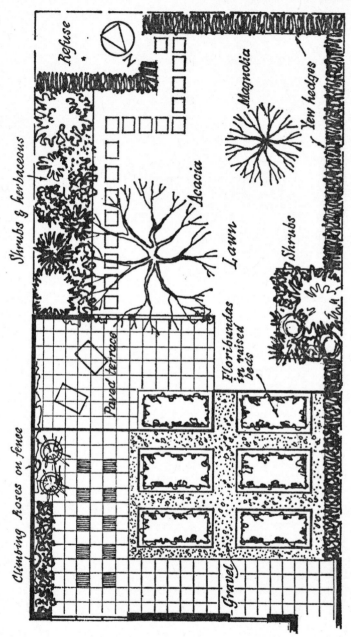

Refuse

N

Shrubs & herbaceous

Magnolia

Yew hedges

Acacia

Lawn

Shrubs

Floribundas in raised beds

Paved terrace

Climbing Roses on fence

Gravel

When designing a rose garden the only rule which can be laid down is the practical one that very small or narrow beds are difficult to plant effectively and very large ones difficult to work. A bed 5 feet wide will accommodate three rows of roses, one 3 feet wide two rows and one 18 inches wide one row. The formal garden shown here in plan and perspective is composed of regular interlocking shapes with beds of floribunda roses enclosed within a paved area or patio. Climbing roses are grown on the wide board fencing. The shrubs, herbaceous and other plants provide spring effects and summer contrast to the roses and include evergreen shrubs to provide interest in winter. This garden and the one on pp. 36 and 37 were designed by Norman H. J. Clarke, F.I.L.A.

without going below the natural level at all by encircling the rose garden with raised beds retained by walls.

Colour Planning or Massing

A question that will have to be decided very early is whether some system of colour planning or massing is to be adopted. Personally, I much prefer to see good-size blocks, each containing one variety, to beds planted with roses of varying height and colour. I would sooner grow eight or ten good varieties suitably grouped than four times that number jumbled together in ones and twos. But it is a matter of taste and one which each must decide for himself.

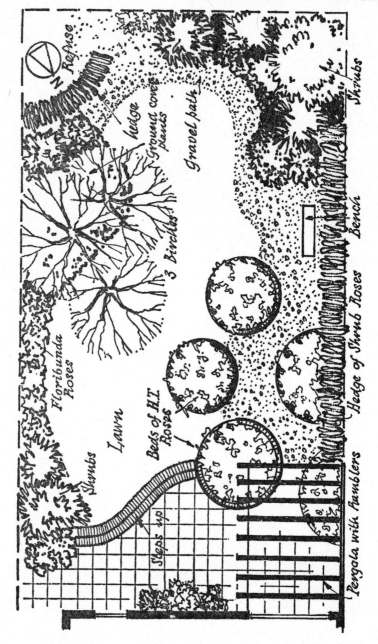

(*Above*) *Rose beds of formal outline have in this garden been happily associated with an herbaceous border, with its different shapes, sizes and colours, and a house on which climbing roses and other wall plants have a congenial setting.* (*Below*) *Bush roses are ideally suited for beds near the house, and floribunda varieties provide a display of colour which lasts from June to October*

(*Above*) *A perfectly proportioned formal rose garden in which the beds are given purpose by the stone plant container. (Below) Standard roses are admirable for planting alongside a path, and in other parts of the garden where colour on a higher plane contributes to the overall design*

The garden shown here in plan and perspective is free-flowing in design and the use of roses must, therefore, be different from that in the formal garden shown on pp. 34 and 35. The circular beds could contain hybrid tea roses which are less formal and solid than floribundas. Rambler roses could clothe the pergola and Rosa rugosa *or one of its varieties could provide the informal hedge beyond this feature. Also some of the rose species should be used in the groups of shrubs for their graceful foliage and colourful hips. Evergreen shrubs and other plants are also needed to provide a background and contrast to the roses*

If colour massing is decided upon, two words of warning are necessary. First, it is dangerous to rely too closely on catalogue descriptions as regards colour. Excellent though the majority of these compilations are, there is a great tendency when it comes to the difficult task of putting into words the precise shade of some novelty to follow blindly like sheep in the steps of a leader. As this leader is almost invariably the raiser of the rose, who rather naturally views his product with the over-fond eyes of the parent, the account of its tints is frequently more flattering to the writer's repertoire of colour names than to his artistic perceptions. Nevertheless, other lists take up the theme, and so we get such errors perpetuated as the description of a glowing pink rose as 'Orient red' or, conversely, a rather crude magenta variety, which requires very careful association, as 'soft cerise'.

Height of Plants

Roses vary in height from the 6 or 8 inches of the minatures to the 15 or 20 feet of some of the vigorous climbers and ramblers. There are shrub roses that will soon make bushes 7 or 8 feet high and as much through, whereas the average hybrid tea or floribunda rose will be no more than 3 or 4 feet. But even within these popular classes of 'bedding' rose there are considerable differences of height and habit. There are dwarf floribunda varieties that are about 18 inches high and tall ones around 5 feet. A really vigorous hybrid tea, such as Peace, can easily attain 5 feet, whereas a smaller kind, such as Pink Favourite, may not exceed 2½ feet.

These are the kind of facts that must be borne in mind when planting roses in the garden, for otherwise it is only too easy to find that a tall variety almost completely hides a shorter one from view. Yet, properly applied, these differences in height can be used to advantage to enhance the appearance of the rose garden, with the taller kinds at the back of borders or in the middle of beds and the shorter ones in front or around.

Path Making

Having settled the general form that the rose garden is to take and the varieties that are to be planted, the next question that must be settled is the material of which the paths shall be constructed. Nothing looks better than grass, and where it is practicable to intersect the rose beds in this way by all means do so.

It must be admitted, however, that in town gardens the grass path is not always desirable. It is essential that the gardener should be able to reach his roses at all seasons of the year. Grass, unless it is growing under ideal conditions, soon gets kicked up, muddy, and altogether horrible, if it is much walked upon in the winter months. For this reason some more durable paving material must frequently be used.

Crazy Paving and Flagstones

Next to grass I prefer either the rectangular York paving slabs or crazy paving. The latter has the advantage that in most districts it is considerably cheaper, but it is rather more difficult to lay effectively. The simplest method is to cut out the paths, removing the turf and soil to a depth of about 1 foot, then fill it with rough clinkers to within a few inches of the surface, and finish off with sifted ashes or sand. The surface should be raked perfectly level. Now set the slabs of stone in this smooth surface, bedding them well down into it, and afterwards scattering sand or fine, dry soil all over and brushing this down into the crevices. After a few heavy showers have fallen it will settle down very firmly, and seeds of suitable plants may be sown in the crevices.

An even more permanent job may be made by bedding the slabs of stone or crazy paving into concrete. Care must be taken that an adequate drainage layer of clinkers and ashes underlies this or much trouble will be experienced in the winter. Water collects underneath the concrete, freezes and expands, exerting terrific pressure upon the solid, unyielding mass, and finally thaws out and leaves great cracks in all directions.

Easily Made Gravel Walks

Gravel makes a very serviceable and attractive path, and is preferable to asphalt or any paving substance which contains tar. No growth can ever be induced upon the surface of a path containing this—a point which may appear a virtue in the mind of the ultra-tidy, but will not appeal to those who, like myself, prefer to see the hard, formal edges of beds softened by the growth of dwarf plants such as violas, mossy saxifrages, arabis, aubrietas, the alpine phloxes and campanulas.

In constructing gravel walks attention must once more be directed to the importance of providing a satisfactory, solid, yet well-drained foundation of rough stones or clinkers and ashes. At least 2 inches of gravel—more if possible—should overlie this. Whether or not this is rolled depends entirely on the type of gravel used. That which contains no sand or finer particles is left loose, merely being raked level from time to time. Frequently such paths as these can be made very cheaply in seaside districts from shingle, or the limestone chippings frequently used for rock garden paths may be utilised. But more commonly gravel that contains sufficient finer particles to enable it to bind tightly when rolled is used for path making. This should be made as solid as possible by ramming and rolling before being used, or considerable trouble may be experienced in preserving a smooth and even walk.

CHAPTER FIVE

Preparations for Planting

Roses are hungry plants and they are likely to remain in the garden for many years. These are both good reasons for preparing the ground well, clearing it of all perennial weeds, which might be very difficult to get rid of once the roses are in, and supplying the soil with the sort of basic food roses like.

If the ground is new and covered with fairly clean turf it may be quite satisfactory simply to dig it, turning the turves grass side downwards in the process. Covered with 8 inches or more of soil, ordinary grass will quickly die and the grass roots in the turf will slowly decay and turn into useful humus. But couch grass, which spreads by stout white underground roots, will struggle up through a foot or more of soil and is a dangerous weed to bury. So are docks, dandelions, bindweed and nettles, all of which have considerable powers of survival. So if the turf contains such weeds as these, or the soil is covered by weeds rather than by turf, it may be better to kill these with chemicals first. This can be done safely by spraying or watering them with either paraquat or diquat, chemicals which kill all green plants they touch but are inactivated by contact with the soil. Two or three days after treatment weeds and grass will have withered and if a second treatment is given four or five weeks later, the weeds can be dug in with much less chance that they will reappear.

If the weeds are not killed in this way the more persistent, such as those I have mentioned, should be picked out while digging proceeds. Do not put them on the compost heap, where they may survive to give further trouble, but destroy them by burning.

For new grass- or weed-covered land a sharp spade is the best tool for digging, but for ground that has already been cultivated and is reasonably free of weeds, a fork will do the work equally well and a good deal more easily. A fork can make all the difference to the working of hard or heavy land, which can be a very tiring task with a spade for those who are not accustomed to using this tool.

It is only necessary to break up the ground to a depth of about 1 foot for it is in this upper layer of soil that the plant gets most of its

The liquid weedkillers paraquat and diquat may be used on ground being prepared for roses. These chemicals can also be used around established rose bushes as long as care is taken to avoid contact with the plants. Always apply in such cases with a watering can fitted with a dribble bar or a fine rose turned with its perforated side downwards

food. Roots may go far deeper for anchorage and in search of water but this they will do quite happily without the soil having been previously dug. But, if soil tends to get waterlogged, deeper cultivation, accompanied by the application of plenty of straw, garden refuse, peat or manure, may improve matters. A cheaper and easier way of doing the same thing would almost certainly be to drain the land (see page 14).

Basic Feeding

It is while ground is being dug that bulky manures can be used most effectively. Spread the material, whatever it is, animal manure, garden compost, peat, shoddy, etc., over the surface as evenly as possible and then, as digging proceeds, it will automatically get turned in. At the same time the surface can be sprinkled with

This sequence of pictures (A to E) shown the correct way to dig. Note the position of the hands and feet at different stages. Ground being prepared for roses need only be broken up to a depth of about 1 foot for the plants get most of their food in this upper layer

coarse bonemeal or, better still, meat and bonemeal or a mixture of bonemeal and hoof-and-horn meal. All these contain much more concentrated plant foods than animal manure, but it is plant food that will be liberated fairly slowly in the soil and so it will keep the newly planted roses well supplied for the first few months. Some of it may even remain for a year or more.

Lime

Lime is only likely to be required if the soil is distinctly acid. This is something that can be ascertained by sending a sample to the county horticultural adviser or to one of the gardening papers, or by purchasing a simple soil-testing kit. Acidity and alkalinity are expressed in terms of the hydrogen ion concentration of the soil water, termed, for short, the pH. In these terms the figure 7 represents neutrality, i.e. a complete balance between acidity and alkalinity. Higher figures show increasing degrees of alkalinity, lower figures increasing degrees of acidity. Thus a soil of pH 6·5 would be very slightly acid and in that respect, if no other, excellent for roses. A soil with pH 5 would be much more strongly acid, perhaps a little too much so for roses, and might benefit from a dressing of hydrated lime at 8 ounces per square yard. It could very well be scattered over the surface immediately after digging has been completed as it would soon be washed in by rain. But I would give no lime to soils of pH 6 or over as an excess of lime can bring problems of its own.

It is a good thing to get all the preliminary ground preparation finished at least a month before roses are planted as this gives the ground time to settle and manures, etc., time to get assimilated. But this interval is not essential and it is quite possible to plant immediately digging is completed and get good results.

CHAPTER SIX

Successful Planting

Roses can be planted in the open ground at any time from late October until the end of March but it is not wise to plant them when the soil is very wet, heavily frozen or covered with snow. In some years and in cold districts this may rule out all January and as least some parts of February. Since autumn planting is to be preferred to early spring planting, because it gives the roses more time to get established before they have to start growing again, it is wise to get as much planting as possible done in November and December.

When the Roses Arrive

Unless the weather is extremely frosty, roses should be unpacked on arrival even if they cannot be planted permanently immediately. If there is to be a delay in planting they can be heeled-in temporarily and will come to no harm for weeks. Heeling-in is a form of temporary planting. A trench, about 1 foot wide and 8 or 9 inches deep, is dug, all the soil being thrown to one side. The roses are lined out close together with their roots in the trench and their stems at an angle away from the displaced soil. Then this soil is thrown back over the roots and trodden down firmly.

If the weather is too cold and the ground too frozen to permit heeling-in, simply open the top of each package so that air can circulate around the rose stems, but leave the packing material around the roots. Then stand the packages in a shed, garage or some other place that is not hot, but is sheltered from the weather. If the roots appear to be dry pour a little water down into the opened packages to wet them. Roses will keep almost as well this way as heeled-in.

Before the bushes are planted any roots which have been badly bruised in lifting must have their damaged portions cut off cleanly with a sharp knife. Also the 'snag', or old brown piece of stock

(*Above*) Roses intended for exhibition which are easily damaged by rain, become slightly scorched or are quickly faded by strong sunshine, should be covered by cone-shaped protectors

(*Right*) If it is desired to hold back a flower, place a wool tie around it a day or so before the show. The wool must not be knotted but simply twisted and pulled gently around the petals

When roses are exhibited in boxes, a special wire support holds the blooms in place

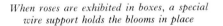

(*Below*) A certain amount of bloom 'dressing' (*manipulation of the petals*) is also permissib but should not be overdone. Here a soft cam hair brush is being used to curl the oute petals on a show bloom

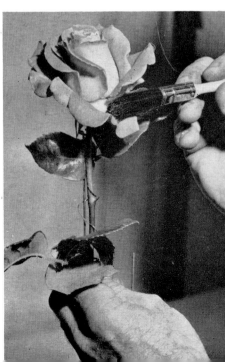

A bowl of roses superbly arranged for competition. Note the evenness of the blooms and that each is so arranged that it stands 'free' for the judges' appraisal

A cup-winning box of blooms. Note the clear identification of the blooms with the name cards held by little wire clips. Naming may not always be insisted on but it is desirable

THE NATIONAL ROSE SOCIETY

A CHALLENGE CUP (Autumn)
for 12 DISTINCT VARIETIES

FIRST PRIZE

about half-an-inch long, which will be found immediately above the point from which all the principal branches issue, should be removed close to the topmost growing shoot unless it has already

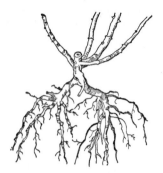

Before planting, roots badly bruised in lifting must have their damaged portions cut off cleanly, as shown on right. Also the 'snag', seen in the left illustration, immediately above the point from which the principal branches issue, should be removed close to the topmost shoot

been cut off at the nursery. This 'snag' is all that remains of the top growth of the stock upon which the rose is grafted.

Distance Apart for Planting

This will vary according to the class of rose to be planted and also to a lesser degree according to variety. Thus very vigorous roses should be allowed more room than weaker ones of the same class, while varieties of erect habit may be spaced more closely than those that branch and spread freely. Speaking generally, bushes of the Hybrid Tea and Floribunda classes may be from 18 inches to 2 feet apart and at least 9 inches from any path. Standards of these classes should be 4 to 6 feet apart, and weeping standards, which are formed from vigorous Wichuraiana or Multiflora roses, 6 to 10 feet. Climbing roses and ramblers should be at least 6 feet apart, and most shrub roses at least 4 feet apart.

The Work of Planting

Let the holes in which the roses are to be planted be made amply wide to allow the roots to be spread out quite naturally without any

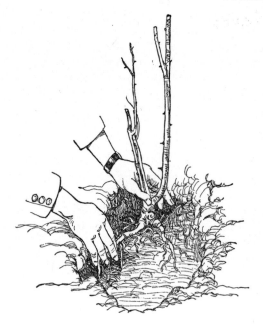

*The planting hole must
be wide enough to allow
the roots to be spread
out naturally without
cramping*

*When nearly all the soil has
been put back in the planting
hole, go round the bush and
make it thoroughly firm with
the foot*

doubling up or cramping. They should be deep enough to allow the union between stock and scion (the point already referred to as that from which all the main growths arise) to be just buried beneath the surface of the soil. This instruction only applies to dwarf, climbing, and rambler roses. Standards are worked high up on the stem, and the correct depth for planting can most readily be gauged by recollecting that the uppermost roots must be covered by at least 3 inches of soil.

Having placed the rose bush in the hole, throw back the soil a little at a time, meanwhile jerking the bush up and down gently so that the particles of soil settle down closely round the roots. It is really much easier if the gardener has someone to hold the bush while he confines himself to filling the hole. When nearly all the soil has been put back, go round the bush and make it thoroughly firm with the foot, unless the soil is very wet or sticky, in which case leave firming until, at a later date, the land is once more in good working condition. But really under such circumstances it is wisest not to attempt any planting at all, but to leave it until better conditions prevail.

Staking and Tying

Standards should be securely staked at once. Indeed it is best to get the stakes driven in before the trees are placed in the holes, as this saves possible damage to the roots caused by driving the stakes through them. Stakes should be stout and long enough to reach up to the top of the main stem after they have been driven at least a foot into the soil. Usually rose stakes are made out of 1 inch by 1 inch deal, cut into 6-foot lengths. They are painted green except for the lowermost 18 inches, which is tarred for better protection against decay.

The ties should be of stout tar twine, and the stems of the trees must be protected from chafing by a piece of sacking, or a strip from an old motor tyre, placed under the string where it would otherwise come in contact with the bark. All ties should be examined periodically to make sure that they have not become too tight and started to cut into the bark. A double twist to the string between the stake and tree acts as a spring, allowing a certain degree of give and take without the tie slipping downwards and saving much damage due to overtight ties.

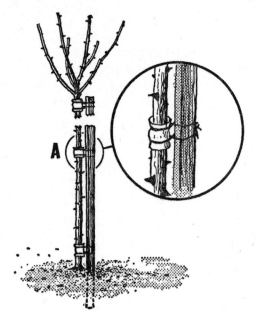

It is best to position the supporting stakes for standard roses before the trees are placed in the planting holes. These stakes should be stout and reach to the top of the main stem after being driven at least a foot into the ground. Make the ties (A) with stout tar twine and protect the stems from chaffing with a piece of sacking or strip of old motor tyre

Winter Treatment

From the time planting is completed until pruning is commenced in the third or fourth week in March, roses require little attention beyond an occasional examination to make sure that they have not become raised and loosened through the action of successive frost and thaw or wind rocked, and that all ties are secure. If they are loosened, tread the soil firmly round them once more.

Planting from Containers

Many nurserymen and garden centres now stock roses in containers of one kind or another. These may be old tin cans, plastic pots, bags made of stout black polythene film, or pots made from specially weatherproofed cardboard or fibre. Whatever the container the object is the same; to enable the roses to be transplanted with a minimum of root and soil disturbance.

If the roses are in tin cans the sides of these must be slit vertically from top to bottom so that each tin can be opened out and the rose, complete with a tight ball of soil around its roots, can be carefully lifted out and placed in a prepared hole. With clean plastic pots it

Mojave (HT)

Wendy Cussons (HT)

Stella (HT)

Virgo (HT)

Tzigane (HT)

Gail Borden (HT)

Buccaneer (HT)

Ballet (HT)

Beauté (HT)

should be possible to remove the plants neatly by inverting them and rapping the edge of the pot on some hard object, such as the handle of a spade thrust firmly into the soil, one hand being held

Planting a container-grown rose. The tin has been slit (this is done at the nursery or garden centre on purchase) and the rose with its ball of roots is placed in the prepared hole. If carefully handled, container-grown plants can be planted at practically any time of the year

under the ball of soil to support it as it slips out of the smooth pot. Polythene bags can be slit with a knife or razor blade and peeled off, and treated paper or fabric pots can usually be torn off in a similar manner.

If container-grown roses can be moved into the rose bed without disturbing the soil around their roots, (and with care this is quite possible) they can be planted at practically any time of year, even in summer when they are in flower. They will suffer no check and will go on growing just as if they had not been transplanted provided they are well watered if the soil is dry.

Obvious advantages of planting from containers are that planting can be done when conditions for work in the garden are much more pleasant than they usually are in autumn or winter, and the roses can actually be purchased in flower so that the buyer can be quite certain that he is getting what he requires. As a rule container-grown roses are not much more expensive than roses lifted from the open ground, but because of the weight of soil around their roots it is uneconomic to send them by rail, and the customer must be prepared to fetch them himself by car or other means.

CHAPTER SEVEN

Pruning Made Easy

Roses have a natural tendency to regenerate themselves by new growths made from near ground level and to get rid of their older stems. This may be observed in wild hedgerow roses which nearly always have some old stems that are dead or dying and plenty of new stems that are full of vigour. What is a natural characteristic of wild roses tends to become somewhat more accentuated in the more highly bred, rather less tough, garden varieties.

The major part of the annual pruning of roses is based on this simple fact. The object is to assist the rose to make strong new

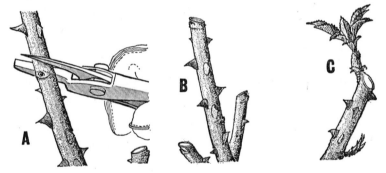

When pruning roses the object is to assist the plants to make strong new growth and to discard old worn-out growth. The pruning cuts are made cleanly immediately above a growth bud (A and B) and it is from buds such as this that the strongest shoots should grow in spring (C)

growth, and to get rid of old, worn-out growth. Once master that, and a good deal of the mystery will already have disappeared from pruning.

Newly Planted Roses

The first pruning a rose receives is always rather severe. This is to concentrate growth on just a few stems so that these can be really sturdy and provide a sound foundation of growth for subsequent years. The best month for pruning newly planted roses is March and if they are actually planted in March it is usually most convenient to prune them just before they are planted. They can then be held in the hand and turned about so that it can be seen quite clearly where each cut is being made.

A young rose bush should have from two to four good stems and the object is to cut each of these down to within 6 to 8 inches of the base. If the stems are examined carefully they will be seen to have little growth buds spaced out along them. These have nothing to do with flower buds, which will come much later in the season. They are the buds from which new shoots will grow, and in winter they are little swellings with a crescent shaped depression and ridge beneath each, the scar left by a leaf when it fell in the autumn. What the rose grower wants is about three of these buds on each stem.

Exactly the same method is adopted with standards, but since the head of branches is on a tall bare stem, the 6 to 8 inches will have to be reckoned to this main stem, not to the ground.

Ramblers and ordinary climbers are cut back in a similar manner and the only exception to hard pruning the first year is with climbing sports. These are pruned more lightly, stems being shortened by about one-third, as hard pruning sometimes makes a climbing sport revert to the bush habit from which it originated.

Established Roses

The first year each rose bush only had two or three stems and each had to be cut back hard. In subsequent years the plant gets bigger and bigger and it will have stems of different age and size.

Moreover, because it is so much bigger and more established, it is not necessary to wait until March before pruning. March is still quite a good month for rose pruning, and many gardeners do all their rose pruning then, but others prefer to spread the work over a longer period and this is quite satisfactory with established roses in all except the coldest places. In these it may be wise to wait until the worst of the winter weather is over, but elsewhere rose pruning can begin in November and continue, as convenient, all winter. If a few buds should be killed by cold there will still be plenty to take their place.

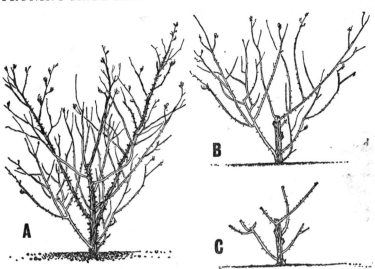

An established rose bush has stems of very different age and size. Before start-
ing to prune note how many good, strong, healthy stems there are and if there
any really old worn out ones (A). If there are several of the former be ruthless
in eliminating the latter (B), and always cut out diseased wood. If big plants
are wanted to make a fine garden display shorten the best stems by a third or
one half and the weaker ones by two-thirds (C)

Before pruning a bush inspect it closely and, in particular, note
how many good, strong, healthy looking shoots it has and whether
it has any really old, worn-out stems. These latter can be rec-
ognised by the colour and appearance of the bark. This will be
rougher and darker than the much smoother, lighter-coloured bark
of the young shoots.

If there are several good young stems one can afford to be
ruthless with the old wood and cut it all out. If there are only one
or two young stems one may have to keep some of the best-look-
ing of the older wood, especially that which is carrying nice new
shoots higher up. If any of the old wood is obviously diseased, with
cracked bark or dark purple or brown decaying patches, it should
be cut out anyway.

Having made up your mind which of this older wood should be
discarded, cut it out. This will probably result in a considerable
thinning of the bush and it will be easier to see what to do next. If

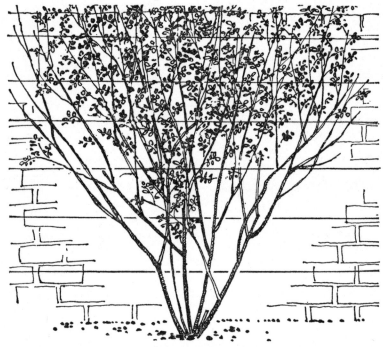

A climbing rose before pruning

the object is to have a good, big plant to make a fine display in the garden, it will be sufficient to shorten the best stems by about a third or a half and the weaker ones by two-thirds.

But if the object is to have roses of the largest size or the highest individual quality it may pay to prune a little more severely; to shorten even the best stems by two-thirds and to take the weaker ones out or at least shorten them to about 6 inches. This harder pruning will result in a smaller plant and fewer flowers but these, individually, will benefit from the reduction in competition.

Climbing Roses

Climbing roses are usually expected to cover a good deal of space and one cannot therefore afford to cut them back as much as bush roses. Yet the same general principles apply and it is just as necessary to cut out really old and diseased stems.

When this has been done, the remaining stems can be retained

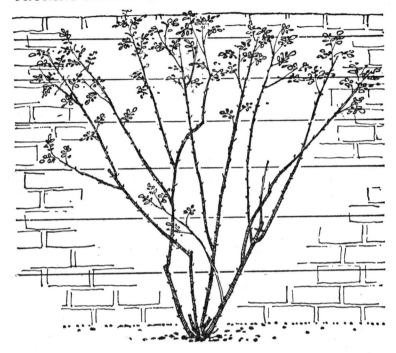

A climbing rose after pruning. Dead, diseased and damaged stems have been removed and the remaining stems retained at nearly full length

at nearly full length, if there is room to train them in, or if there is not, they can be cut back to fit them to the available space.

If some of the stems that are retained have side growths which have produced flowers (the remains of these, or some heps may remain to indicate this) each such side shoot should be cut back to an inch or so. This is both tidy and it helps the rose to make more flowering side shoots the next year.

A few varieties, such as Paul's Scarlet Climber and some of the climbing sorts, do not naturally make sufficient new growth from low down. To rectify this an occasional strong stem can be cut back to within a foot of ground level to encourage branching.

Rambler Roses

Exactly the same methods are applied to ramblers as to climbers and the only additional point of any importance is that some

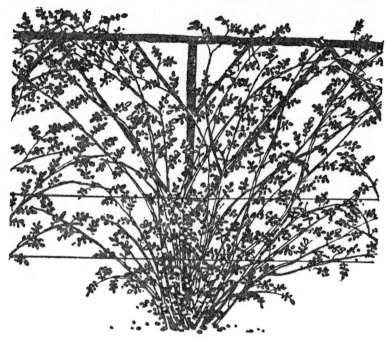

Rambler roses are pruned in the same way as climbers except in the case of such varieties as American Pillar, Dorothy Perkins, and Excelsa which habitually make very strong new growths from quite low down

All stems more than a year old on ramblers of the latter type (see above) can be cut out at the end of the flowering season

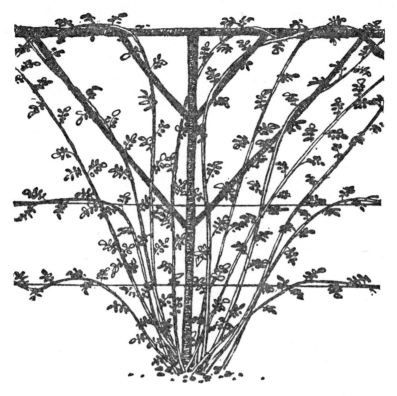

The young stems should then be spaced out to cover the available area

ramblers, such as American Pillar, Dorothy Perkins and Excelsa, habitually make so many strong new growths (canes might be a more appropriate description) from quite low down, that all stems more than a year old can be cut out annually. The easiest way to do this is to prune ramblers in September or early October as soon as they have finished flowering. The faded flowers will still be there and every stem that is carrying faded flowers can be cut out. That will leave nothing but young stems and these can be trained in at full length. Other varieties such as Alberic Barbier, make less basal growth and with these it is necessary to retain some of the older stems, cutting each of these back to a point at which a strong young stem grows from them.

Weeping Standards

These are formed from ramblers which are budded high up on a strong brier stem. The long stems are then trained spirally downwards on special wire training hoops much like old-fashioned crinoline frames. These are themselves nailed or tied to stout stakes driven into the ground close to the brier stems. Pruning of these weeping standards is similar in principle to that of the same

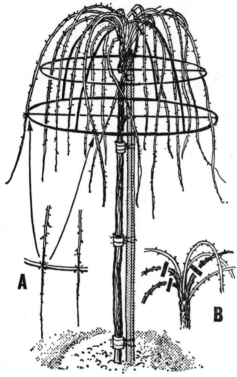

Weeping standards, which are formed from ramblers, are pruned in a similar manner to the same roses grown as ramblers, but it is done rather more severely. The long stems are trained downwards and tied onto the special wire training loops (A). More old worn wood is cut out (B) and young canes shortened or reduced in number if they take up too much space on the frames

roses grown as ramblers, but it is rather more severe. More of the old wood is cut out and the young canes are themselves shortened or reduced in number if they occupy too much space on the crinoline frames. The object is to keep these frames well-furnished, but not overcrowded, with healthy young growths.

Standard Roses

Standard roses are simply bushes perched on a long bare stem, to make them look like little trees. The head of a standard is pruned just like a bush rose, the old and diseased stems being cut out first and then the younger stems shortened, the best by a third or a half, the weaker ones being removed or cut back by two-thirds or three-quarters.

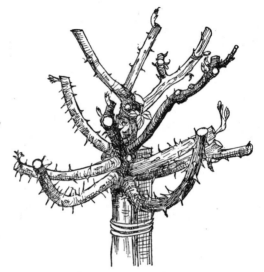

The head of a standard rose is pruned in exactly the same way as a bush rose. This specimen has been hard pruned

Shrub Roses

The principles of pruning shrub roses are still the same, but since they are so much bigger and stronger growing, it is not necessary to be so meticulous in shortening the younger stems. Often it is quite sufficient to cut out the really old or diseased branches annually and then, every third or fourth year, to give a further fairly drastic thinning of the younger stems to keep the bushes from becoming over-crowded and losing vigour.

Summer Pruning

In order to keep a rose bed tidy it is necessary to remove faded flowers fairly regularly in summer. While doing this it is a good plan to prune the bushes a little; not simply to cut off the faded

When removing faded rose blooms prune the bushes a little at the same time. Take off 5 to 10 inches of stem

blooms, but to take 5 to 10 inches of stem as well. Examination will show that those varieties that flower all, or most of, the summer are making new shoots from lower down. These are the ones that will carry the later flowers and they must be retained. But the old flowering stems can be removed as far back as these new shoots, or, if there are none, as far as a leaf which has a fat growth bud at the point where its stalk joins the stem.

CHAPTER EIGHT

Summer Care

Immediately after pruning, established roses (i.e. all roses not in their first year in the garden) should be fed. If they can have some rotted animal manure as well as chemical fertiliser, so much the better, but animal manure can be difficult to come by. If it is unobtainable something should be used in its place that will supply humus. This can be well-rotted garden refuse or good peat or any of the other humus-forming substances I have already named.

Whatever it is, manure, compost, peat, etc., it is spread over the surface of the bed, not dug in. To dig around established roses is to risk injury to their roots. The most that can be done now is to prick the surface an inch or so deep with a fork. It is because of this difficulty in subsequent cultivation that the initial cultivation of rose beds should be done thoroughly.

Whatever bulky, humus-forming material is used, the roses will almost certainly need some more concentrated feed. This can be in the form of meat and bonemeal, fish guano, hoof and horn meal or a compound chemical fertiliser. Personally I think it is wise to ring the changes, for what is missing in one application may be supplied by another. But every rose grower tends to acquire his own theories on this subject and it probably does not much matter what is used so long as the roses are adequately fed. They are hungry plants and nitrogen, phosphorous and potash are the plant foods they are most likely to run short of. That is why a balanced rose fertiliser can be so useful for it will contain all three of these chemicals in reasonable ratio.

Spraying

Black spot is an almost universal disease of roses in country districts, though town dwellers often see little of it. It is a disease that can be kept in check by spraying, provided this starts early enough, and April is the correct month in all but the coldest, most backward parts of the country. What to spray with I have discussed on p. 84 and all I am concerned with here is to emphasise that spraying must start early and be continued at fairly frequent intervals all summer.

Greenfly can be troublesome from about May onwards but can be controlled very early by systemic insecticides (see p. 81). Mildew is unlikely to appear before midsummer, when dinocap may be used to check it, but caterpillars and sawfly larvae may be active well before that date. Spraying with DDT, lindane or malathion will keep them under control.

Thinning

Rose growers who are keen on exhibition may find it worth their while to thin the young shoots that appear within a week or so of pruning. They may decide to keep only one new shoot on each pruned stem and to rub all the rest out with the thumb. But this is seldom necessary or desirable when roses are grown primarily for garden display, for which purpose all the new shoots can be left to develop into flowering stems.

Disbudding

When roses are grown for exhibition or to provide specimen blooms, rather than to make the biggest possible display in the garden, it is necessary to disbud the flowering shoots, and leave only one bud to a stem. The strongest terminal bud is the one which should as a rule be preserved, the weaker side buds being removed as soon as possible with a sharp knife. The only exception is with certain very full roses, such as Conrad Adenauer and Karl Herbst, which sometimes produce coarse flowers from the terminal buds. In that case one of the best of the side buds should be kept on each main flower stem. This work should be attended to regularly twice or thrice a week throughout the flowering period. For very large blooms the number of flowering stems is also restricted, but this is a subject to which I shall return later in the chapter on roses for exhibition (see p. 68).

Note particularly that disbudding is not necessary for the health or well-being of the plant, and is only carried out to get bigger and finer blooms. It is never necessary with cluster roses such as the Polyanthas, Floribundas, Wichuraianas, Multifloras, Musks, etc.,

A typical flower shoot of a bush rose

nor with any of the species. Even the large-flowered types may be left to flower naturally if the main object is a big splash of colour in the garden. The quality of individual blooms is then less important than their number.

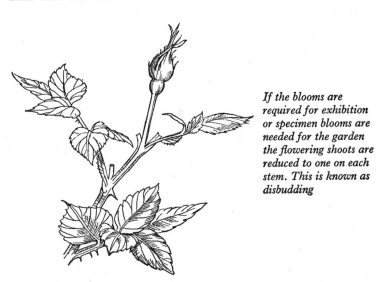

If the blooms are required for exhibition or specimen blooms are needed for the garden the flowering shoots are reduced to one on each stem. This is known as disbudding

Summer Feeding

Roses are such hungry plants that, even when they are growing in good soil and have been well manured and fed in spring, they usually benefit from two or three more applications of fertiliser between June and August. For this purpose such things as meat and bonemeal and hoof and horn meal are not much good as they are too slow acting. Readily soluble chemicals, such as sulphate of ammonia, superphosphate of lime and sulphate of potash, are required and these are the usual base ingredients of general garden fertilisers or special summer rose fertilisers. These mixtures (not the separate ingredients) are sprinkled on the surface of the soil, usually at 2 or 3 ounces per square yard, but manufacturers' instructions should be consulted.

Weeds and Weeding

Weeds must not be allowed to compete with the roses and one way to prevent this is by mulching. This is the term applied to any fairly thick dressing spread over the soil surface. For roses, lawn mowings and peat are two very suitable mulching materials and an inch-thick layer of either, maintained more or less from spring to autumn, will reduce weed competition considerably.

An alternative to mulching is hoeing and this has the merit that, by stirring the surface soil and breaking it up, it leaves the rose beds looking very tidy. A dutch hoe is the best tool to use as this leaves the hoed soil untrodden on, flat and even. If the beds are not too wide they can easily be hoed from the paths or grass surrounds. Only if the ground is hard or the weeds are very tough may a draw hoe be found to be a better tool than the dutch hoe.

A third way of dealing with weeds is by the use of weedkillers and some of these may actually be used in conjunction with a mulch. Best for this purpose are paraquat and diquat, both liquids which must be applied from a watering can fitted with a dribble bar or a very fine rose turned with its perforated side downwards. But if either of these chemicals is used great care must be taken not to get them on to the rose leaves for they will kill these just as effectively as they will kill weeds. Hold the dribble bar or rose low, so that the weedkiller is delivered direct to the weeds below the level of the rose leaves. It will not harm the hard stems, though it may harm

Karl Herbst (HT)

Violet Carson (Flor)

Gold Crown (HT)

Korona (Flor)

Allgold (Flor)

Masquerade (Flor)

Chanelle (Fl

young stems that are still green and soft. It will do no damage to roots as it is inactivated by the soil.

Yet another weedkiller which may be serviceable to the rose grower is simazine. This is applied, not to weeds, but to the surface of ground previously cleared of weeds. On this it forms a film which will kill any seedling weeds that attempt to grow through it.

Simazine will not kill persistent weeds, such as dock, dandelion, bindweed and couch grass, but if these appear in simazine-treated beds they can be killed by individual treatment with paraquat or diquat. Hoeing cannot be used effectively in conjunction with simazine since it breaks up the film of chemical and destroys its efficacy.

Suckers

As explained in the next chapter, most purchased roses are produced by a form of grafting known as budding. Each plant consists of two different roses, a wild rose, or 'stock', which supplies the roots, and a garden rose, or scion, which provides the branches and flowers. The nurseryman is at pains to cut off all the top growth of the stock long before he sells the plant, and often that is the last one sees of the stock above ground. But sometimes it tries to reassert itself and throws up fresh shoots direct from the roots. If these are allowed to remain they will produce nothing but flowers of their own kind, usually small, worthless, single flowers totally unlike those of the garden rose the stock is supporting.

So one important summer task for the rose grower is to watch for suckers. Once one has been shown a sucker alongside a garden rose it is easy enough to recognise, yet it is extremely difficult to describe a sucker in words. For one thing they are not all alike, as nurserymen use different kinds of rose as stocks. The wild brier stock, or Canina, has smaller leaves of a rather greyer shade of green than most garden roses. The Rugosa stock has thinner, rougher leaves and great quantities of small spiny thorns. The Laxa stock is small leaved and so is the Multiflora.

The best advice that can be given is to view with suspicion any growth that seems to differ in character from others in the rose bed and to trace it right back to its source. If it grows from one of the known rose stems it is good rose growth. If it comes straight from the roots it is a sucker. If it does neither, but seems to come direct from the main stem of the rose where it enters the ground, the task is more difficult. One must ascertain whether it grows from a point above or below that where scion joins stock; that slightly swollen

Remove sucker growths from rootstocks as quickly as possible. If necessary, remove the soil around the plant with a trowel until the base of the sucker is uncovered. Then cut it off as near as possible to the main stem for if a stump is left more suckers will arise

union to which I referred when discussing rose planting (see p. 47). If it comes from above the union it is good rose growth, if from below it is stock and an undesirable sucker.

All sucker growths from rootstocks must be removed as quickly as possible. It may be necessary to use a trowel to dig away the soil until the base of the sucker is revealed and it can be cut off, without leaving any stump to produce two or three more suckers where only one existed before.

Suckers from roses grown from cuttings or layers are harmless as they have exactly the same character as the rest of the bush (see p. 72).

CHAPTER NINE

Roses at Flower Shows

Probably few gardeners start to grow roses with the idea of exhibiting them but because of the great number of horticultural societies, some local, others attached to offices or factories, many gardeners soon find themselves contemplating the possibility of exhibiting.

Classes for Beginners

At small shows the standards are not usually very exacting and any reasonably well-grown rose has a chance of winning a prize. There are usually classes for individual flowers, for several flowers shown in one vase, for two or three sprays of floribunda roses and perhaps for a vase of roses unrestricted as to the number of blooms but most likely restricted as to size of base. All these are good classes for a beginner to test his skill and learn the basic arts of showing.

More Complex Classes

But if he later decides to graduate to one of the national shows he will find himself up against much stiffer competition and more complex classes. Some will be for specimen roses shown in boxes. This is a very old method of exhibiting and still one of the most exacting as each bloom is separately displayed on a board or 'box' which makes it virtually impossible to conceal any fault. The size of these boxes is laid down in the rules, the top or display board to be 12 inches wide and 18 inches deep for 6 blooms, 33 inches wide by 18 inches deep for 12 blooms, and 3½ feet by 18 inches for 36 blooms. These boards are slightly tilted, so that the blooms are well displayed. There are holes in the board 6 inches apart and into these are put metal tubes which are filled with water and hold the blooms.

Roses to be exhibited on boards can be cut with fairly short stems, say from 6 to 8 inches, but for exhibition in vases at these national shows long stems are required up to 2 feet, and they must be stiff and strong. Before launching out as an exhibitor in any of these shows it is wise to go and look very closely at the exhibits and talk to some of the old hands who are usually quite pleased to be asked for advice and to show a novice how it is done.

What the Judges Look For

As specimen blooms, whether at local or national shows, it is almost entirely hybrid tea varieties that are shown. Nor are all the hybrid teas equally suitable. What the judges look for is size, fullness and good shape combined with freshness and freedom from blemish. Some varieties that are excellent for garden display have flowers too small or too lacking in substance for exhibition. It is equally true that there are some varieties grown almost exclusively for exhibition since they lack the good habit of growth or freedom of flowering expected in garden roses. But those are varieties for the specialist. There are plenty of dual purpose roses for the gardener who wants a nice-looking garden as well as a few good blooms to exhibit.

In order to get extra size of bloom and length of stem exhibitors usually prune rather more severely than is necessary for garden display only. They will cut even the strongest stems back to 4 or 5 inches and eliminate weaker stems altogether and when new growth starts in the spring, they may rub some of it out keeping only a limited number of stems per plant so that each grows strongly. When the flower buds appear they will certainly remove all but one on each stem, usually retaining the central bud unless it is damaged or deformed. This they will do quite early while the buds are still small so that the side buds do not draw away food from the bud that is to develop into an exhibition bloom.

Some roses are readily damaged by rain or become slightly scorched or are quickly faded by strong sunshine. To prevent this keen exhibitors make use of cone-shaped protectors which can be purchased for the purpose. These are attached by wire clips to sticks or canes on which they can be easily slid up or down. The stick or cane is pushed firmly into the soil so that it is conveniently close to the bloom to be protected and the cone protector is secured in position like a dunce's cap an inch or so above the developing flower.

Another Show Tip

Another show tip is to place a wool tie around each flower a day or so before the show. Natural coloured or white wool is used, not dyed wool lest it stain the petals. It is not knotted but simply twisted and pulled gently around the petals to hold them together and prevent the flower opening too fast. A 'blown' rose which shows a hollow or open centre is no good for exhibition. Roses should be cut and placed in water immediately. If they can be taken to the show in water, so much the better, but if this is impossible they should be left in water for an hour or so, then be taken out, their stems wiped and packed flat in clean, paper-lined boxes. Immediately on arrival at the show they should be unpacked, ½ inch cut from the bottom of each stem, and placed back in water.

It is wise to take more blooms than will be required and make the final selection when actually staging. Freshness and freedom from blemish are first essentials. Next comes shape, substance and size, roughly in that order. Good shape in a hybrid tea means that it is at the peak of development, full grown but not starting to fall open and become flat. The centre should be high and pointed. A bad fault easily overlooked is a deformed or 'split' centre or a centre that falls away instead of standing up. A little manipulation of the flower known as 'dressing', is permissible but can easily be overdone. The expert, by very gently squeezing the centre of the flower, particularly if it is a slightly immature flower, will force the outer petals to open a little and give a more pleasing shape to the bloom. If one or two of the small outside 'guard' petals are badly weather damaged they can be removed but judges will quickly note and penalise any serious removal of faulty petals. Sometimes a soft camel hair paint brush is used to make some of the outer petals curl slightly, which again adds to the appearance of the flower.

Blooms that hang on thin stems are bad. The stem should be stiff and sturdy and leaves should be healthy and undamaged.

If some blooms have been tied with wool these ties may be left until a few minutes before the exhibitors have to leave the exhibition hall or tent. They will help to hold the flowers in peak condition for the judges. But do not forget to remove them for the judges are unlikely to give any awards to tied flowers.

Studying the Schedule

Before entering any show study the schedule carefully—not only those paragraphs that refer to the particular class or classes you intend to enter but also the general rules which apply to exhibits as a whole. If there is any point you do not understand ask for an explanation before the exhibit is staged. The stewards at most shows are able to answer most questions but if still in doubt go to the secretary. It is far better to get questions answered first and not have protests and misunderstandings after the show.

Make quite certain you know how the flowers are to be staged, in vases or boxes, singly or several together. Classes for floribunda or climbing roses usually specify a certain number of stems or sprays. This sometimes causes confusion. A spray includes all the flowers that come naturally in one cluster. It does not mean a whole main branch with several side growths each carrying its own spray of flowers.

At some shows it is a rule that each flower or variety must be named. This is usually done by printing the name clearly on a small card (a visiting card cut lengthwise in half will do) and standing this at the foot of the vase. Tubes for boxes have little wire clips into which the name cards are slipped. But even if the schedule does not insist on naming it is worth doing as it always pleases the judges.

Finally, do not enter in too many classes or in too ambitious classes until you have had a little experience. It is more encouraging to do a few simple classes well than a lot of difficult ones badly.

CHAPTER TEN

Rose Propagation

Few are the gardeners who are prepared always to purchase their plants or beg them from more enterprising friends. At first the rose-growing novice may feel disposed to leave such a difficult-sounding process as 'propagation' to those who are more advanced, but it will not be long before he will be wanting to try his skill at raising a few roses.

As with most garden operations, the essential thing in the successful propagation of roses is painstaking care over each detail. It is not sufficient for the actual operation of putting in the bud or making the cutting to be done correctly. If the preliminary work has been scamped or subsequent treatment is carelessly attended to, the result is almost sure to be disappointing.

Cuttings

The simplest method of propagation for the beginners is by means of cuttings. All the wild (or species) roses, most vigorous shrub roses, including the old-fashioned varieties, and all rambler roses are readily increased by this means, while some of the polyantha, hybrid perpetual, hybrid tea, and floribunda varieties can be raised quite satisfactorily from cuttings. These are inserted during September and October, and are made from ripened wood produced during the preceding summer. If pieces of young growth can be pulled off with a 'heel' of the previous year's wood they will be found to root more readily. The 'heel' should be neatly trimmed up with a sharp knife and the shoot shortened to about 6 inches. Should it be impossible to obtain such cuttings with a heel, select well-ripened shoots and cut them cleanly across immediately below an 'eye' or bud. Then shorten the tops so that the finished cuttings are from 8 to 12 inches in length.

The cuttings are firmly planted in shallow trenches which are nicked out with a spade. Make one side of this trench as nearly vertical as possible and stand the cuttings against this 2 inches distant one from each other. The trench should be 3 inches deep. A little gritty sand scattered along the bottom will be of great help in encouraging the cuttings to root. The soil is now pushed back into the trench and made thoroughly firm round the cuttings. Do not be afraid to press hard with the foot. Loose cuttings are almost sure to fail. If the weather is very cold a little straw scattered among them will serve as a protection. The following autumn they should be lifted and planted in nursery beds, the rows being 18 inches one from the other and the rooted cuttings 1 foot apart. The following spring they must be pruned hard back to within 2 or 3 inches of ground level and will be ready for their permanent quarters by the next autumn.

An alternative way of dealing with rose cuttings is to take them in July, preparing them from firm young stems, such as those that are removed with the faded flowers, and to insert these either in a mist propagator or in sandy soil in a pot which is then placed inside a polythene bag. These cuttings are not prepared with a 'heel' but are severed cleanly just below a leaf, which is itself removed. The base of the cutting is dipped in hormone rooting powder before insertion. Such summer cuttings root very quickly and by August or September can be potted singly and placed in a frame or greenhouse for the winter, to be planted out the following spring.

One merit of roses grown from cuttings is that any suckers they produce are of the same kind as the cuttings and will produce flowers of the same colour and quality. Their suckers, in fact, instead of being a nuisance, are a positive benefit, to be encouraged because they supply the bush with just the kind of healthy young growth it needs.

Rose cuttings. These are inserted in September or October and are made from well-ripened wood produced during the previous summer. A, If possible select young wood with a 'heel' of the previous season's wood attached but if this cannot be arranged select well-ripened shoots for this purpose, as shown. B, Remove the lower leaves. C, Make a clean cut immediately below a bud and shorten the top so that the cutting is from 8 to 12 in. long. D, The cuttings are planted in prepared shallow trenches which are then filled in and the soil well firmed with the feet

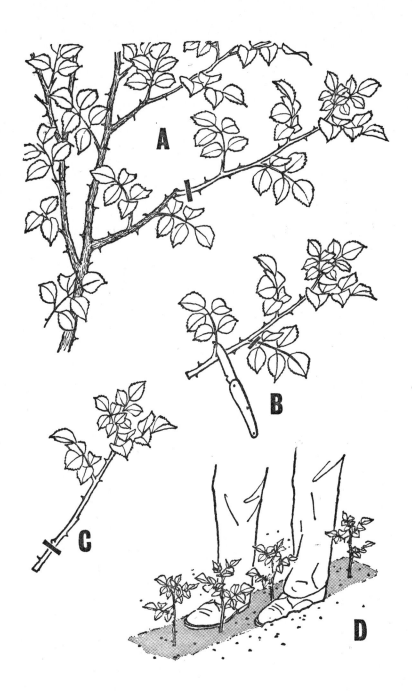

Budding

Although many vigorous growing roses are better on their own roots, the majority of garden hybrids give the best results when budded on a suitable stock. The wild dog rose of our own hedgerows, *Rosa canina*, is that most favoured, though numerous other varieties and species are used. Sweet brier, *R. rugosa*, *R. laxa*, *R. manetti*, *R. multiflora* and *R. polyantha* are a few of those utilised, some being of special service under certain conditions. But the amateur will be most interested in the dog rose, which can be counted upon to give good results and plants that will bear high-quality blooms for a number of years. Rugosa stocks are very easy to work and they encourage vigorous growth, but they produce suckers very freely and are not so long lived as brier.

Raising the Stocks

Dog-rose stocks may be raised from seed or cuttings. If it is required to raise them from seed the heps are placed, during the autumn, in sand in shallow boxes and stood where they will be exposed to frost but are secure from mice and voles. In the spring the fleshy covering will have decayed and it will be a fairly simple matter to separate the seeds. It is not necessary to get each seed entirely clean so long as they are sufficiently separated to enable them to be sown fairly evenly. Sand and seeds are sown together in shallow drills in the open. By November the young seedlings should be sturdy enough to be transplanted to the beds where they will be budded. Place them in rows 2 feet apart and allow 6 inches between the plants.

Rugosa stocks can also be raised from seed in the same way, but are rarely satisfactory as they encourage coarse growth. Cuttings give more satisfactory results, and these, together with cuttings of the dog rose, are raised precisely as described for garden roses, and should also be planted 2 feet by 1 foot apart at the end of the first season's growth in readiness for budding. The following March the young stocks are cut to within 2 inches of the ground.

For standard roses suitable brier stems are cut early in November from hedgerow plants. A stout pair of leather gloves, a pair of good secateurs, and a really strong spade are necessary for this task. Straight stems about the thickness of a walking-stick and not so old as to have entirely lost their green appearance are best for the purpose. Chop them from the parent plants with as much root as possible. Then, when sufficient have been obtained, they must be trimmed up. Any damaged portions of root and useless old stumps and also any side growths are removed, and the stems themselves shortened to 5 feet. A few extra stout briers may be left longer for weeping standards, while the shorter ones will come in useful for half-standards. Plant these stems 1 foot apart in rows 3 feet wide.

Standard rugosa stems are produced under special conditions in large nursery beds devoted to this purpose, and no attempts should be made to produce them at home. As a rule they can be purchased quite cheaply in the autumn.

In the following spring each standard stem will throw out a number of lateral shoots. All these may be left on rugosa stocks, as they serve to draw up sap through the main stem and keep it pliable. Buds are inserted directly into this main stem at the height desired for the head of branches, which is usually 5 feet for full standards and 3 feet for half standards.

Budding on to the main stem is not possible with dog-rose or brier standards, as the bark is too thick and hard. In consequence, all except three of the new side growths are rubbed out. Select these three at the height required for the head of the finished tree. It is into the bases of these laterals that the buds are inserted.

With bush and climbing roses the bud is put into the main stem of the stocks as near the roots as possible, whether they are brier or rugosa stocks. With this end in view, when budding time arrives, the soil is drawn away from the base of the stock with a hoe and trowel so that the incision may be made just below ground level.

Inserting the Buds

The actual operation is the same for both bush and standard roses. The gardener should obtain a special budding knife for the purpose. This will have one good blade and a thin ivory handle for opening the bark. During July or August, select a half-ripened shoot of the current year's growth from the rose which it is desired to propagate. A reliable test for the ripeness of the wood is made by breaking off the thorns with the thumb. They should snap off cleanly, but the wood exposed must appear green and juicy. If it is dry and hard the shoots are too ripe. Should the thorns refuse to break off, but instead bend and tear, the wood is not sufficiently mature.

Having selected a shoot, remove all the thorns and cut off the leaves, leaving only the footstalk of each. Also discard the thin end of the shoot. Now insert the knife about ⅜ inch below a bud and make an upward cut coming out the same distance above. The gardener has now a single bud or 'eye' with a piece of bark enclosing a small portion of wood, and the footstalk of the leaf which makes a convenient handle to hold it by. The small piece of wood at the back must be carefully removed with the point of the knife and the fingers.

Assuming that the gardener has satisfactorily managed the first part of the operation, he must next make a T-shaped incision in the bark of the stock, being careful not to press too hard on the knife and so cut down into the wood. The bark is carefully lifted with the flattened ivory handle of the knife, and the bud inserted. It is then bound in position with a piece of raffia, care being taken to start this tie below the lowest point of the incision and carry it well above the top of the T.

After three weeks the bud should be examined. If the stock has swelled much and the raffia is pressing hard on the bud, it must be cut and if necessary retied. But in all probability by this time the bud will have taken and will be able to look after itself. Should the portion of the bark carrying the bud still be green and not yield to gentle pressure it has made a union. Later on the bud will plump up, and may even start into growth, though 'shot eyes,' as these first summer's shoots are termed, are not very desirable. They usually suffer more heavily during the first winter than buds that have remained dormant.

The following March the stocks are cut back with a pair of sharp secateurs immediately above the T-shaped incision. With dog-rose

---

The technique of budding: A, A half-ripened shoot of the current year's growth is chosen, all the thorns are removed and an upward cut is made from about ⅜ in. below a bud to the same distance above it. B, The small piece of wood at the back is carefully removed. C, Shows the bud (a) with the wood removed (b), D, The top end of the bud is then trimmed with a knife. E, A T-shaped incision has been made in the bark of the stock. F, The bark is lifted carefully with the ivory handle of the budding knife and the bud inserted in the opening. G, The bud is then bound in position with raffia

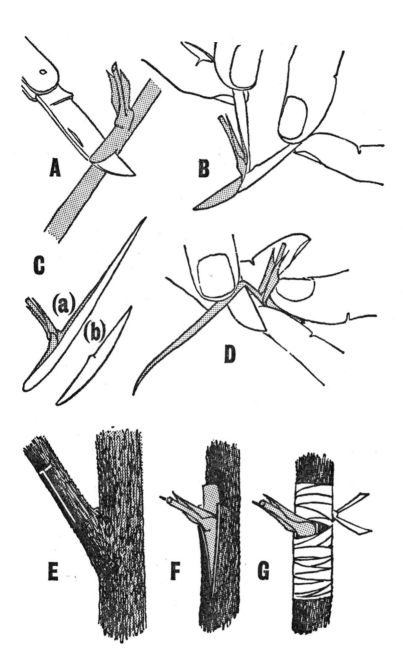

standards the side shoots bearing the buds are shortened in the
same way. Shot eyes are pruned back to about two dormant buds
each. If all has gone well, and the buds have not perished during the
winter, they will presently start into growth, and by the autumn
will have produced strong rose bushes ready for the permanent
beds.

Layering

Some roses, and in particular the more vigorously growing ramblers,
may be increased readily by means of layers. Young shoots are bent
down during the summer months, sliced half through at a joint in
an upward direction, and this cut portion placed in the soil and held
in position by a wooden peg or large stone. The shoot will form
roots from round the cut, and later may be severed from the parent
plant and put in where required.

Seedling Raising

Seedling raising is a very fascinating hobby, but should only be
carried out where definite crosses have been made. So many roses
are introduced each season that it is not desirable that their number be swelled by chance and inferior seedlings. But if the amateur
rose grower wishes to embark upon cross-fertilisation of roses, by
all means let him do so. He should first carefully study the peculiar-
ities of each variety and pick his parent plants accordingly.

The flower chosen as the female parent should have the petals
very carefully removed while still in bud, after which the anthers are
cut off with small nail scissors. Out-of-doors it will be necessary to
cover each prepared flower with a white muslin or paper bag but
breeding is best done under glass and, if this is regularly fumigated,
individual protection is usually unnecessary. The stigmas become
slightly sticky when ready to receive pollen from the male parent
and this fertilisation can be effected by removing the petals from a
well-developed flower and dusting the ripe anthers over the stigmas. Soon heps should begin to swell and these are left to ripen
when they are gathered and the seeds carefully removed.

The actual process of seed sowing and rearing is the same as that
described for the dog-rose stocks.

CHAPTER ELEVEN

Pest and Disease Control

Having said so much about the beauties of the rose and the pleasures of rose growing it seems a pity that it is necessary to speak of foes and difficulties. Yet these exist and must be faced. The rose is no more immune from the unwelcome attentions of insect pests and the ravages of disease than any other plant, and the rose grower who wishes to enjoy the best possible results from his plants must make himself acquainted with the chief among these, and the remedies to be employed against them.

Firstly he must learn to detect an attack at the earliest possible moment. Only in this way can he preserve himself from much trouble. If an attack is dealt with before it has taken hold of the plant, it may generally be crushed with comparative ease. But once let it get a grip and it will take a great deal of eradicating.

How to Spray

When applying liquid insecticides and fungicides it is important that the spray should be reasonably fine. The foliage and growth must be thoroughly covered with a thin film of fluid which must not run into large drops. Do not fail to wet the underside of the foliage thoroughly. Much trouble has its real seat here, and if only the more accessible upper surface of the foliage is sprayed, little good will result. Some chemicals used for spraying are poisonous and if they fall on food crops these should not be harvested within the period recommended by the Ministry of Agriculture. This should be stated on the container.

There are many forms of apparatus which are suitable for applying sprays. The simplest is the garden syringe. It should be provided with a nozzle that will give a fine but driving spray and have a bent neck to facilitate spraying underneath the leaves. Another handy type where only a limited number of bushes have to be treated is the hand pneumatic sprayer, which looks something like a blow-lamp and has, in fact, a similar air-tight container in which pressure can be raised by means of a small hand pump.

Where a considerable area has to be treated a bucket or knapsack sprayer may be used. Either will be useful for many other jobs besides the spraying of rose bushes. Winter washing apples, summer spraying fruit trees, tomatoes and potatoes, and the lime washing of poultry houses, may all be done with these serviceable machines.

PESTS

Greenfly

The most universally troublesome pest with which the rose grower will have to contend is the aphis or greenfly. The tiny green female insects may make their appearance quite early in the spring. They will first of all be clustered on the tender growth at the very tips of the shoots. As the attack increases—and the rate at which greenfly can reproduce themselves is simply astounding—they will spread to the under surface of the leaves and cause them to cockle and curl. The simplest way of dealing with greenfly is with systemic insecticides. These are chemicals which, instead of remaining on the outside of leaves and stems, enter into the sap and make it poisonous to some of the insects which suck it.

Three good systemic insecticides are available to rose growers: menazon, which only kills greenflies and other species of aphis; dimethoate, which kills, in addition to greenflies, caterpillars, red spider mites, leaf hoppers, and capsid bugs; and formothion, which also kills red spider mites and leaf hoppers but is only claimed to kill small caterpillars. All three are available, under brand names, as liquids ready to be diluted with water as advised by the manufacturers. Since they are carried round in the sap, it is not so

---

Rose pests: A, Thrips, a very small but active pest which can be troublesome in a hot, dry season. It feeds on the sap and attacks the flowers and leaves. B, Cuckoo spit, a yellowish insect which protects itself with a mass of froth. C, A leaf hopper and leaves damaged by this pest. The damage shows as faint white mottling. D, The leaf rolling sawfly causes the leaves of roses to form long, narrow coils. E, Greenfly (aphis), the most universally troublesome pest of the rose. F, Rose slugworm, a pest which attacks the upper and lower surface of the leaves and turns these eventually into transparent skeletons

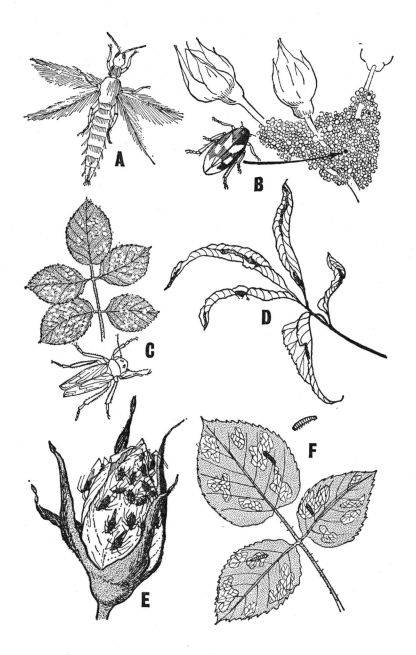

A

B

C

D

E

F

necessary as with non-systemic insecticides to wet all the leaves. When in a hurry I have often applied them from a watering can fitted with a fine rose, a somewhat wasteful method but very quick and easy.

Leaf Hoppers

These are also known as frog flies. They are small pale yellow insects which live on the undersides of the leaves and suck sap from them, as a result of which the leaves become faintly mottled with white. The insects shed their skins as they develop and often the empty white skins are the most certain way of confirming the cause of the mottling, which looks much like that caused by red spider mites. The systemic insecticides dimethoate and formothion (see Greenfly) will also kill leaf hoppers, or the roses may be sprayed with malathion or DDT.

Cuckoo Spit

There are usually only a few of these little yellowish insects about but they protect themselves with a mass of froth, so they can be quite conspicuous. Malathion or BHC will kill them if it can be brought into contact with them, but this is difficult because of the protective covering of froth. This can be removed by heavy syringing with water, but it is often quicker to go over the bushes by hand, searching for and destroying the cuckoo spit insects.

Red Spider Mite

Another pest which may occasionally attack roses, particularly if they are growing in a very hot and dry spot, is red spider mite. This popular name is rather unfortunate, as the creature is not a spider and bears no great resemblance to one. It is certainly reddish, but is so minute that unless the gardener has very keen sight or is provided with a good hand lens, even this part of the popular name is of little aid to identification. Red spider is a pest belonging to the 'mite' class. Like the aphis and frog-hopper, it lives by sucking the juices of plants.

An attack may most readily be detected by a patchy yellowing of the leaves. If such an appearance is noted, the lower side of the foliage must carefully be examined with a magnifying glass. Should minute reddish insects be detected, immediately spray the bushes with malathion, dimethoate, formothion or derris, in accordance with the manufacturers instructions.

Sawflies and Other Caterpillars

The larvae or grubs of several species of sawfly may do considerable damage to roses. One of these lives and feeds in the pith, boring its way into the interior of the shoots, and causing them to turn yellow and wither. Another eats the surface of the leaves, but leaves the parchment-like skeleton. These are often known as slugworms. Yet a third rolls the leaves up into long, narrow coils. If their presence is suspected a careful search should be made, leaves being turned up or unrolled as necessary. The caterpillars are quite small and may be yellowish, greenish or black in colour. With the pith-boring sawfly the only course is to cut off and burn all infected shoots. The leaf gnawing and rolling species may, however, be destroyed with derris, BHC or DDT. Many proprietary insecticides based on these chemicals are available.

In addition to the sawflies, the larvae—i.e., caterpillars—of many moths feed upon the leaves of roses. No useful purpose would be served by describing them in detail, as the treatment for each is alike. Hand picking will account for many, while if papers are spread under the bushes and they are vigorously shaken a number of caterpillars will fall off and may easily be gathered and destroyed. Apart from these direct methods, the bushes may be sprayed with the same insecticides as suggested for sawfly larvae.

Thrips

In a hot, dry season thrips may be very troublesome. They are very small, long in proportion to their width, active, and in colour anything from yellowish to nearly black. They feed on the sap, particularly favouring the opening flower buds and their effect on these is to check their development, disfigure them and cause the edges of the petals to turn brown as though scorched. If thrips are suspected carefully pick a damaged flower and shake or tap it sharply over a sheet of white paper. The insects will fall out and, though so tiny, can easily be seen running about on the paper. The plants should be sprayed with DDT, lindane, malathion or nicotine.

DISEASES
Mildew

In addition to the insect pests, the rose grower will have to keep a watch for several fungoid diseases which may attack and do a considerable amount of harm to his roses. The commonest, and one which if it commences early may be very damaging, is rose mildew. This usually makes its appearance towards the end of the summer, and is worst in closed-in, stuffy gardens. Some roses are very liable to mildew, and should not be planted near trees or where they will be much shaded by walls.

Mildew looks like a grey powdery coating upon the foliage. If the attack is a bad one, the leaves will become much cockled and misshapen and may even fall prematurely. Once again let me urge the necessity for early measures to be taken against the trouble. Where the disease gets hold of the plants no amount of spraying will cure it. At the first signs of the powdery meal upon the foliage, or even before in the case of roses known to be specially liable to mildew and in shut-in gardens, spray the plants with dinocap, or with thiram, a chemical sold under various proprietary names. It must be used as a spray according to manufacturer's instructions.

Black Spot

Another fungoid disease which is often rampant towards the end of the season is that known as black spot. This has the appearance of more or less circular dark blotches upon the leaves. Certain varieties are very susceptible to the trouble. The fungus is usually more difficult to eradicate and more serious in its results than mildew. Trees may become badly defoliated and, in the course of a few years, so much weakened that they succumb entirely. Preventive spraying with captan will check the disease. All badly affected leaves must be picked off and burned. In addition, all fallen leaves must be swept up and burned in the autumn. When the trees are

---

Rose diseases: A, Black spot, a disease which is often rampant towards the end of the season. B, Rust, which appears on the leaves as rusty, raised spots of an orange colour. C, Mildew, which is worst in closed-in, stuffy gardens. D, Canker, a trouble which shows first as reddish or purplish patches and eats into the bark until it is destroyed and may crack. E, Die-back, which attacks year-old branches during the winter, causing die-back from the tip

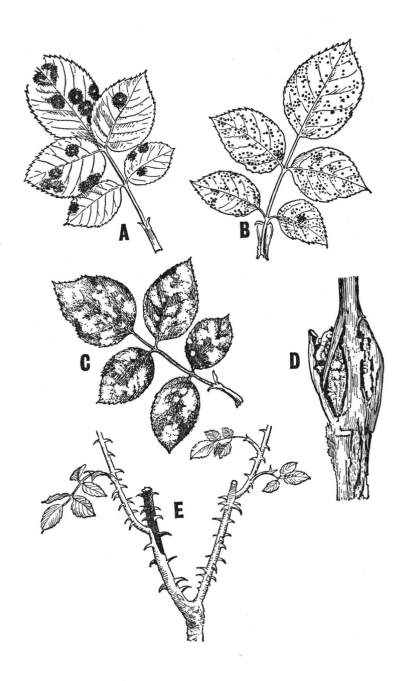

quite bare, spray them with copper sulphate, 1 ounce per gallon of water. Remove and dispose of the surface soil. In April spread a thick mulch of dry grass clippings over the whole bed and add to this as necessary, but never disturb it. Preventive spraying with captan should be continued from April to September inclusive at about fortnightly intervals.

Rose Rust

This disease has increased greatly in some places and is believed to be spread by certain stocks, notably *Rosa laxa*. Its name describes it very well, for it appears on the leaves as rusty raised spots of an orange colour.

Spraying with zineb or thiram or colloidal copper should begin in June if this disease has been troublesome, for, as with black spot, prevention is easier than cure.

Rose Stem Canker

Like apple canker, this disease attacks the branches of the bushes and eventually encircles and strangles them. At first the disease shows on the younger wood as reddish or purplish patches. These extend and the disease eats into the bark until it is eventually destroyed and may crack. Sometimes large calluses form round these cracks, giving the wounds a festering appearance.

All diseased wood should be cut out and burned. Frequent summer spraying with one of the fungicides recommended for black spot and winter spraying with copper sulphate may do some good, but generally canker proves well-nigh incurable.

Die Back

This attacks the year-old branches of roses during the winter, causing them to die back from the tip. Some varieties appear to be more susceptible than others, and certainly poorly ripened growth is most likely to suffer. It is probable that many supposed cases of die back are simply due to weather damage, but disease organisms are also involved.

Preventive steps which may be taken include the use of fertilisers containing plenty of phosphates and potash, which tend to ripen and harden the wood; avoiding feeding after mid-August and accidental injury to the bark; thorough thinning of overcrowded growth so that what is left gets plenty of light and air; and autumn spraying with Bordeaux mixture or colloidal copper.

Crown Gall

Very large, irregular and roughened swellings sometimes appear on rose stems, especially near soil level. These are known as crown galls and are caused by bacteria. They do not apparently cause much damage though they look very unsightly. They should be cut off in the autumn and the wounds coated with Stockholm tar.

Index

Note:—Roses are indexed under species or variety
Abbreviations:—d = line drawing, p = photograph facing page given